Engaging Fathers in the Early Years

A Practitioner's Guide

Also available from Continuum

Communication, Language and Literacy, Nichola Callander and Linday Nahmad-Williams

Do Parents Know They Matter?, Alma Harris, Kirsty Andrew-Power and Janet Goodall

Knowledge and Understanding of the World, Linda Cooper, Jane Johnston, Emily Rotchell and Richard Woolley

Leadership Skills in the Early Years, June O'Sullivan

Personal, Social and Emotional Development, Pat Broadhead, Jane Johnston, Caroline Tobbell and Richard Woolley

Engaging Fathers in the Early Years

A Practitioner's Guide

Edited by Carol Potter
and Roger Olley

continuum

Continuum International Publishing Group

The Tower Building	80 Maiden Lane Suite 704
11 York Road	Suite 704
London SE1 7NX	New York NY 10038

www.continuumbooks.com

British Library Cataloguing-in-Publication Data
A catalogue record for this book is available from the British Library.

ISBN: 978-1-4411-9695-8 (paperback)
       978-1-4411-5785-0 (ePub)
       078-1-4411-1069-5 (PDF)

Library of Congress Cataloging-in-Publication Data
Engaging fathers in the early years: a practitioner's guide / edited by Roger Olley and Carol Potter.
    p. cm.
  Includes bibliographic references and index.
   ISBN 978-1-4411-9695-8 (pbk.) – ISBN 978-1-4411-5785-0 (ePub) – ISBN 978-1-4411-1069-5 (PDF) 1. Father and infant–Great Britain. 2. Father and child–Great Britain. 3. Father and infant. 4. Father and child. I. Olley, Roger. II. Potter, Carol.
  BF720.F38E54 2012
  649′.10851—dc23
                          2011040986

Typeset by Fakenham Prepress Solutions, Fakenham, Norfolk NR21 8NN
Printed and bound in India

To Chris Whittaker with love and thanks

CP

To Dee and Siobhan, we got there in the end

RO

Contents

Note: The word 'agency' has been used throughout the book as an umbrella term for all organizations, teams and other groups working within the early years.

Acknowledgements

We would like to thank several people who have been important in the development of this book. Thanks to Chris Whittaker who provided great support throughout the project, with many helpful suggestions at critical moments. We would also like to acknowledge the contribution of the whole Fathers Plus team, past and present, who have undertaken such excellent work over a number of years and from whom we have learnt so much. Finally, we would like to remember Joy Higginson, without whom fathers work in the North-East would not have been developed.

Notes on Contributors

Charlotte Dack is the Workforce Development Coordinator for Children North East Fathers Plus, UK. She has a background in education and family learning and was instrumental in developing the Fathers Plus Service and launching and coordinating the National Family Man Schools Outreach Programme.

Tim Kahn worked for eight years with the Pre-school Learning Alliance – one of the major providers of early years services in England – where he coordinated work to include fathers in childcare settings. His two children, who are now 26 and 24, taught him the importance – and the joys – of hands-on fathering as far back as the 1980s. Since then he has campaigned to promote men as carers, long before its importance was widely recognized.

Bev Keen worked as a teacher of primary aged children for more than a decade and is now a Senior Lecturer at Leeds Metropolitan University, leading a teacher training course.

Kevin Lowe worked for the Trust for the Study of Adolescence/Young People in Focus, UK, for eleven years as Assistant Director and Co-Director, where he had specific responsibility for its training, practice development and publications work. Kevin led two major national projects on developing practice in supporting young fathers and established the website Supporting Young Fathers Network www.youngfathers.net.

Liz McDonnell is a Senior Research Fellow at the UK Council for Psychotherapy. She has worked on a range of research projects focusing on health, education and family issues. She has a particular interest in young fathers and worked on the Talking Dads project – a participatory research project exploring the experience of young fatherhood.

Roger Olley is a freelance consultant. He was the Head of Service in Father Work for Children North East, UK, and was responsible for the development of the nationally recognized Fathers Plus Service. Roger has over 30 years' experience of working in health, social care and voluntary settings. He has extensive experience in developing parenting work on a multi-agency basis. Roger acts in a consultancy and advisory basis to many organisations, both regionally and nationally, who are seeking to develop or extend their working with men and fathers. He is the co-author of the accredited 'Developing Men Friendly Organisations' course. Roger was awarded the MBE for services to families in 2011.

Carol Potter is a Senior Lecturer in Childhood and Early Years at Leeds Metropolitan University, UK. She worked in a variety of social care and education settings with disabled children for over ten years, first as a residential social worker and then as a teacher, before moving into higher education. Carol lectures in the areas of disability, communication, and men and early childhood, and has a range of research interests including autism, the development of early language and communication, reflective practice and working with fathers. Carol was the joint author of a book called *Enabling Communication in Children with Autism* and has recently published in the field of father engagement in disadvantaged areas.

Geoff Read is a freelance consultant and the author of www.separated-familiesmatter.org.uk – a child-centred resource for UK professionals. He designed a multi-agency approach on separated parenting and on fathers for Rochdale Metropolitan Borough Council, UK, integrating strategy and practice based on the Gender Equality Duty. Geoff also chaired the Rochdale Separated Parenting Steering Group. He is currently working with children in Fukushima, Japan.

Kathy Rist is currently the Regional Manager for Contact a Family, covering the North East of England and Cumbria. She has worked with disabled children and their families in the statutory, penal, business and voluntary sectors and has a wealth of experience. For the last three years she has been the strategic lead for parent participation through Aiming High for Disabled Children across the North East and Cumbria and has been actively involved in the formation of parent forums, encouraging partnership working between parents and professionals with tangible and acclaimed mutual benefit.

Nigel Sherriff is a Senior Research Fellow in the Centre for Health Research (CHR) at the University of Brighton, UK. He is a member of the British

Psychological Society (BPS) and is a Chartered Psychologist and Chartered Scientist. Dr Sherriff is also the author of *Supporting Young Fathers: Examples of Promising Practice*, and has a wide range of research interests including young fathers and parenthood, (international) health promotion, and public health.

David Van der Velde is Business Support Manager at the regional charity Children North East and Director of the technology company Consult and Design International. He spent over six years developing and managing the Fathers Plus service.

Gary Walker is a Principal Lecturer in Childhood and Early Years at Leeds Metropolitan University, UK. He has worked in a variety of social care settings with and for children and families for over 20 years, including as a social worker, child protection education co-ordinator, and children in care education coordinator for a large education authority. His publications include a sole-authored book *Working Together for Children: A critical introduction to multi-agency working*, an edited volume (with Phil Jones) *Children's Rights in Practice*, as well as chapters for edited volumes covering safeguarding and looked-after children.

Introduction

The purpose of this book is to raise awareness amongst practitioners of the importance of including fathers in service delivery, the difficulties involved in doing so, and approaches to overcoming these challenges. It focuses specifically on engaging fathers in their children's early years for two main reasons. First, the evidence suggests that if fathers are engaged early, they are more likely to remain so later on and whatever services can do to support that engagement is therefore of great significance. Second, research shows that positive father involvement early in children's lives is strongly associated with more beneficial outcomes for children later on (Flouri and Buchanan, 2004).

There is now no doubt that the positive involvement of fathers in their children's lives promotes better child well-being in a number of key areas. Following a review of 24 studies, Sarkadi et al., (2008) concluded that father engagement:

> reduces the frequency of behavioural problems in boys and psychological problems in young women; it also enhances cognitive development while decreasing criminality and economic disadvantage in low SES areas (p.157).

It is important to state that when we talk about 'fathers' throughout the book, we are referring to biological and other father figures/male carers, except where explicitly stated otherwise.

A key strategy for promoting greater father engagement is the timely and effective provision of support to men in their parenting role. However, despite an increasing policy and statutory focus in this area, it remains the case that almost all formal family support is offered to mothers, with the result that the vital contribution which fathers can make may be undermined in a number of ways.

Despite the convincing research that demonstrates the importance of fathers in children's lives, the field of father/male carer inclusion is a challenging one, with services traditionally experiencing great difficulties in delivering services to men. We will explore why this is the case and offer a number of well-validated approaches for recruiting and retaining father participation in services. A key theme throughout the book will be that a gender-differentiated approach is essential to achieve effective father engagement. In straightforward terms, such an approach acknowledges that the needs of men and women are likely to differ in a number of significant ways and that to work effectively with men, services will need to address these needs differently. At present, children's services are generally geared to meeting the needs of women which goes a long way, it is argued, to explaining the relative lack of involvement of men.

It is important to state clearly that not all father involvement is positive for children and families, for example, where there is domestic and/or child abuse. A key message for services, though, is that for good or ill, fathers do have a significant impact on their families. This book is primarily aimed at practitioners working within universal services. Whilst it is vital that services work effectively with those men who may pose risks for their families, much more specialized approaches will be needed in such circumstances and these are beyond the scope of this book.

The book is divided into three parts. The first explores a range of topics that contextualize the issue of father inclusion. Chapter 1 provides an evidence-based rationale for working with fathers, summarizing some of the key research findings in relation to positive father involvement and child outcomes. Chapter 2 gives an overview of the development of United Kingdom (UK) policy in relation to fathers, and details service responsibilities in relation to engaging fathers across children's services. Chapter 3 sets out a systems approach to collecting information on fathers which, it is argued, is the very first step on the road to father inclusion.

Part Two of the book explores issues relating to father inclusion across a range of early years services in the antenatal and post-natal periods, early years play settings, and in the early transition from such settings to formal education. Barriers to inclusion are discussed in depth, together with detailed approaches for overcoming these obstacles.

Part Three introduces notions of diversity in fatherhood. Fathers are by no means a homogenized group and both similarities and differences must be taken into account to provide accessible services to a range of fathers whose experiences and needs may differ in significant ways. It would, of course, be impossible to cover the full range of diverse experience in one volume. Here, we will be exploring specific issues relating to working with young fathers,

fathers from black and minority ethnic communities, fathers of disabled children and separated fathers. There are a number of barriers to service use that generally affect all fathers, but in these chapters, issues which are specific to these groups will be examined, together with approaches to developing effective service delivery. Case-study material will be provided to illustrate ways forward.

Each chapter includes key issues for reflection so that individuals and, more importantly, teams of practitioners can reflect upon the issues raised in relation to their own organization and begin to explore ways of implementing and evaluating any changes necessary to improve the involvement of fathers in service delivery.

Finally, we would wish to emphasize that this is not a book about fathers *per se*, nor does it seek to undermine the absolutely vital contribution that mothers, or female carers make to children and family life. Rather, it starts from the assumption that positive father involvement in children's lives, supported by effective service delivery, contributes significantly to the well-being and development of children and families and that this aspect of support for families has, for too long, been significantly overlooked.

Part 1
Overview

1

Why Involve Fathers?

Carol Potter

Introduction

In recent years, there has been an increasing focus in the United Kingdom (UK) on fatherhood and supporting the role of fathers in children's lives. In 1996, Burgess and Ruxton, commented that 'fatherhood is on the agenda as never before' (p. 23). In 1998, New Labour acknowledged the importance of fathers in the Green Paper, 'Supporting Families', stating: 'Fathers have a crucial role to play in their children's upbringing' (Home Office 1998, p. 50). In the following decade, an increasing number of policy frameworks were introduced which specifically emphasized the need to involve fathers in family services. Such policies and their implications for practitioners will be discussed in more depth in the next chapter.

Why has this been the case? Why such a focus on the importance of fathers in their children's lives and why now? There are two main reasons. The first relates to the major changes in family life which have occurred during the last 30 years which have seen a much greater number of mothers going out to work, leading to fathers becoming increasingly involved in the day-to-day care of their children (Featherstone, 2009; Stanley, 2005, for example). The second relates to a large body of research which demonstrates that children benefit in a number of important ways when fathers are positively involved in their lives. It is this second issue which we will address in this chapter.

Father involvement: benefits for children and families

One of the key reasons for the increased focus on fathers in policy has been the research demonstrating that when fathers are positively involved in their children's lives, children benefit in all kinds of ways. Having said this, it is important to reiterate Lamb and Lewis' (2004) key point that men's relationships with their children need to be understood within the wider network of family relationships. It has been shown that not only do men influence children in their relationships with them but also fathers affect mothers' behaviour and attitudes and vice versa, with children's behaviour also affecting parents. What we are seeking to highlight here is research which specifically emphasizes father impact on child outcomes, an issue which has only recently become better understood, while acknowledging that these impacts take place within a wider family context, in which, of course, mothers also play a key role. The salient point here is that while the role of mothers has always been acknowledged as fundamental to child development, the role of fathers very often has not.

The field of research in relation to father involvement and child outcomes is now wide-ranging and complex and it is beyond the scope of this chapter to review it in great depth here. What we will do is to:

• highlight key research findings for practitioners
• suggest how and why these are important
• discuss the implications of research findings for early years service delivery.

Fathers and benefits: what is the evidence?

Eirini Flouri stated that the 'discovery of the father has been one of the major themes in child developmental research in the past 30 years' (2005, p. 18). Before that time, research on child well-being focused largely on the relationship between mothers and children, with fathers being seen as on the margins of family life. Attachment theory (Bowlby, 1953), in the early days, was concerned only in terms of children's attachment to their mothers. However, the increased focus on fathering and child outcomes, has highlighted a range of positive benefits related to positive father involvement in children's lives. For example, Sarkadi and colleagues (2008) analysed 24 studies which looked at father involvement and outcomes for children. They found that 22 of the 24 studies showed positive results; they concluded that father engagement:

> reduces the frequency of behavioural problems in boys and psychological problems in young women; it also enhances cognitive development while decreasing criminality and economic disadvantage (p.157).

These findings, however, relate to biological fathers. There is still much to learn in relation to child outcomes and other kinds of father-figure engagement, such as stepfathers.

Below, we will briefly review some of the most important evidence in relation to father involvement and child outcomes in the early years.

Effects of father caring in the first year of life

An important study by Washbrook (2007) explored the impact of paternal care on babies and young children under 3, using a large sample of over 8,000 children. One interesting finding was that extensive paternal care during a child's first year had little or no measured impact on children's later educational outcomes when they started school. This would seem to run counter to widely held beliefs that during the first year of children's lives, mothers have a uniquely important role to play.

Fathers' impact on children's language development

Some studies have considered how the language used by fathers and mothers in their children's early years might impact on their later language development. One important study by Pancsofar and Vernon-Feagans (2006) involving 67 families, analysed the talk used by fathers and mothers in free play settings with their 2-year-old. The study found that fathers who talk to their children at 24 months made a 'unique contribution to children's later expressive language skills at 36 months' (p. 582).

Educational achievement

Moving on to the school years, Rebecca Goldman conducted a wide-ranging review of research in the area of father involvement in their children's learning (see Goldman, 2005). She examined five high-quality studies on father involvement and child outcomes and concluded that greater father interest and involvement in their children's school and learning is statistically associated with a range of better educational outcomes for children, including:

- better school attendance
- better exam results
- better behaviour
- higher educational expectations
- better social and emotional outcomes for children.

(Goldman, 2005)

These outcomes were independent of the mothers' contribution. Such results are clearly significant and bear further reflection, especially in the light of other research which shows that resident fathers are less likely than resident mothers to be involved in their children's schools. In addition, other groups of fathers, especially those from poorer areas, are less likely to be involved, with the result that their children are further disadvantaged. This issue will be explored further below.

Father involvement, disadvantage and child outcomes

For a number of years, it has been accepted that there is a strong link between poverty and educational disadvantage. There is overwhelming evidence that children from poor backgrounds do significantly less well educationally than children from advantaged areas. The Joseph Rowntree Foundation's annual report on 'Monitoring Poverty and Social Exclusion' (Parekh et al., 2010) found that 11-year-old pupils entitled to free school meals were twice as likely *not* to reach the basic standards in English and Maths, as those not on free school meals. The key issue is clearly that those with higher qualifications go on to gain higher incomes while those with few qualifications do not and this has been identified as one of the key mechanisms for the continuing lack of social mobility in the UK.

We have seen that positive father involvement leads to better child outcomes, but what is the situation with regard to fathers of children from disadvantaged backgrounds? Fathers from a lower social class are *less likely* to be involved in children's out-of-school learning and education than fathers in more advantaged areas (Flouri and Buchanan, 2003), often due to their own poor educational experiences. Fletcher and Daley (2002, p. 4) stated:

> Fathers [are] also more likely than mothers to report a history of school failure in literacy, a dislike of reading aloud and the use of strategies to shorten the time spent on reading with their children.

In an important study in 2006, Blanden took a slightly different approach to investigating social mobility. We know that poor children are likely to become poor adults, to a large extent because of low educational attainment. However, some children from such backgrounds do escape from this cycle and Blanden was interested in finding out what enabled them to do so. A number of factors were found to be important, one of which related to father involvement. The study found that where fathers from disadvantaged backgrounds were involved in their children's education and learning, children were more likely to escape from poverty later on. This is an extremely important finding and leads to the question: how then, can we best support greater father involvement in children's education in poor areas? Chapter 6 reports on a project which was successful in achieving this, engaging fathers in their children's early learning through a children's centre and then in the reception class at their local primary school.

Key issues for reflection

- To what extent were you aware that positive father involvement has been shown to improve outcomes for children?
- Does this affect your view of the importance of working with fathers in any way?

Having discussed the compelling research which demonstrates the ways in which positive father involvement benefits children and families, it is important to highlight the fact that very often images of fathers in our society do not accurately reflect such a state of affairs. Such images undoubtedly contribute to an often-prevailing 'deficit model of fathering' in which men are often seen as unable or unwilling to nurture their children, of which more below.

Perspectives on fathers: images of incompetence

Within the media, both film and print, fathers have often been portrayed as incompetent and/or unwilling to care for their children. For example, in the popular 80s film *Three Men and a Baby*, while the men involved ultimately became competent in caring for a baby, the fact that they are able to do so was viewed worthy of Hollywood film-making and in addition, all of the promotional literature used to market the film projected images of incompetence. A striking exception during the 70s and 80s was *Kramer versus Kramer*, released in 1979, which was viewed as groundbreaking in making a case for fathers being as capable of caring for a child as mothers.

More recently, in 2009, The Fatherhood Institute carried out a survey of images of fathers in 'soap operas' on television in an average week. Results showed that fathers were shown to be five times less involved in family life than mothers and they were much more likely to be portrayed negatively. Mothers were depicted as the linchpin of the family, while fathers were shown mostly as in and out of family life and generally incompetent in the care of their children. In addition, a BBC4 documentary *Men about the House* (2010) reviewed the ways in which prominent father figures have largely been treated as figures of fun over the years in major television shows such as *Steptoe and Son*; *Some Mothers Do Have 'em*; *The Simpsons* and *The Royle Family*.

Fathers have not fared much better in the print media, with perceptions of men often distorted in terms of the proportion of negative, as opposed to positive, images presented. For example, in a survey of a range of newspapers, Lloyd (1994) found that while mothers were generally shown as ordinary people doing ordinary things, fathers were depicted in more extreme terms as heroes/monsters: abusers; saviours; breadwinners or defenders.

In response to the often-negative images of fathers projected, Hawkins and Dollahite (1997) argued that fathering has often been seen as a role which men generally perform inadequately. Commentators have used terms such as a 'deficit model' of men or 'a role inadequacy perspective' to describe the way in which men have often been represented. As we shall see in the next chapter, such a stance has also been reflected in public policy until the last decade.

These negative images and stereotypes are important since, given the all-pervasive influence of the media, they may have contributed to the widespread attitudinal barriers which stand in the way of services actively supporting fathers in their parenting role (Goldman, 2005). This overemphasis on 'dangerous', incompetent and irresponsible fathering, it is argued has served to obscure the wider experience of the majority of fathers whose contributions have been demonstrated to result in positive outcomes for children.

Professionals who start from more positive assumptions about the influence of fathers can be said to be espousing a 'generative' model of fathering (Hawkins and Dollahite, 1997), believing that fathers and male carers are capable of nurturing the next generation.

Key issues for reflection

- From your own experience how do you feel that fathers are currently portrayed on television and in the newspapers? What is the balance of positive versus negative images?
- To what extent does your service espouse deficit or generative approaches to fathers? How would you evidence this?

Fathers and benefits: implications for services

It is clear then that positive father involvement in children's lives can have a range of beneficial impacts. What has this to do with service provision for families? Put simply, the more that fathers can be supported in their parenting role by the whole range of family services, the more likely it is that these benefits will flow to both families and children. This would seem to be especially the case in situations where fathers are struggling with the role, for a variety of reasons, such as low self esteem, often linked to disadvantage and poor educational experiences. However, and this is the principal rationale for this book, it remains the case that family and educational services are generally offered to and taken up by mothers, as will be demonstrated below.

Levels of father involvement in services

There is significant evidence that despite the manifest importance of fathers in children's development, fathers are much less engaged in family and education services than mothers. In 2001, The National Family and Parenting Institute (Henricson, 2001) reported that fathers are 'not perceived to be in the mainstream of provision and [face] barriers to support' (p. 7). The National Audit Office (2006) found that children's centres were found to be '*less effective at meeting the needs of fathers*' (p. 34). Similarly, a major study by Page et al., (2008) which was commissioned by the Department for Children, Schools and Families (DCSF), now the Department for Education, surveyed 46 local authorities and concluded that:

> Father inclusive practice was not seen to be routine or mainstream in family services (Page, Whitting and McLean, 2008, p. 6).

There is also strong evidence that fathers are much less involved in family learning programmes. In 2009, Ofsted surveyed 23 providers of such programmes and found that they were 'generally unsuccessful in recruiting many fathers and male carers' (p. 6). With regard to father inclusion in early years health services, Quinton and colleagues (2002) found that young men often felt excluded from involvement with antenatal and post-natal care by health service professionals and, further, that health care professionals themselves reported knowing little about the fathers, did not see them as central to their task, and felt they lacked the skills to engage with men.

In the next section, we will look at how this situation can begin to be addressed. The following themes and issues will be further discussed later in the book.

Father inclusion: the need to raise awareness

We will now shift the focus from exploring issues relating to research on the benefits of father involvement to the ways in which this research could be used in relation to service development. As we saw above, despite the many benefits of positive father engagement in their children's lives, it remains the case that fathers are not regularly engaged or included in a range of family-related services. One of the most important starting points for addressing this situation is to raise staff awareness by introducing staff training on working with fathers and the very first issue to address within such sessions is: why involve fathers? The introduction of research at this point showing how father involvement benefits children is often the most effective way of beginning to shift perceptions around the importance of working with men.

Roger Olley has extensive experience of training practitioners in the area of fathers work and has found almost universal surprise with regard to the research on father involvement and benefits for children and families. Many, if not most practitioners are unaware, first that such research exists, and second, that it is so wide-ranging and compelling.

Key issues for reflection

- How could you introduce staff training on working with fathers in your setting?
- How could the research identified above be used in staff training?
- What kind of challenges could the introduction of such material give rise to?

The kinds of issues which are most often raised in response to research on the benefits of father involvement are discussed below, together with possible approaches for responding to them.

What about abusive fathers?

As stated above, we need to be clear that not all father involvement benefits children. There is clear evidence that children from homes where there is marital violence, for example, are at high risk of developing problems in several areas: emotional, psychological, health, social and cognitive (see Holden and Barker, 2004 for example). Similarly, physical or sexual abuse of children by fathers or father figures has a number of extremely damaging effects on children.

The key issues to note in relation to training, however, is that fathers who perpetrate such acts against children and partners are in the minority and that it is important to explore the extent to which services can work with such fathers to produce better outcomes for children. We must emphasize again at this point, that this book is intended for practitioners working within universal services, who will refer men to specialist services when necessary.

Benefits of father involvement: what does it mean for lone mothers?

Another issue which can sometimes arise when a focus on the benefits of father involvement is presented, relates to implications for lone mothers. This is without doubt a sensitive issue and one which needs to be addressed with care. The first point to make is that there is considerable diversity of child outcome even within the same two-parent family, demonstrating that a wide range of influencing factors are likely to be involved in children's development, in addition to the contribution or otherwise of a father figure (Flouri, 2005). This means that children in lone-parent families, led by a woman or a man can achieve well, depending on the quality of the parenting they receive from that parent, as well as a range of other factors. The need to highlight the link between father involvement and child outcomes is partly as a result of the almost complete absence of such a focus before, as previously indicated in relation to the ways in which the media and previous governments have conceptualized the role of fathers in families. The issue is, that we cannot ignore evidence relating to the benefits of father involvement on child outcomes but as professionals, we need to approach the issue with sensitivity when working with lone mothers.

Conclusion

The relative lack of father inclusion in a range of services, especially in the early years will be demonstrated throughout this book, together with a range of evidence-based approaches for working towards greater engagement of men within them. Research findings in this chapter have shown that the more that men can be supported in their parenting role by a range of family services, especially in the early years, the more likely it is that children and families will benefit in the future. A recent UN report (2011) argues strongly that much greater support for fatherhood is needed globally:

> First and foremost a social policy environment is needed that stimulates and enables specific actions to promote fatherhood and the engagement of men by the media, services, civil society organizations and the private sector (p. 74).

Summary

- Positive father involvement in children's lives results in better outcomes for children and families.

- Father involvement can be enhanced through the provision of effective support to men in their parenting role.
- However, the vast majority of formal family support is generally offered to and taken up by mothers, especially in areas of disadvantage.
- Evidence relating to father involvement and child and family outcomes can be used productively in staff training sessions to introduce a compelling rationale for ensuring that staff see the benefit of working with fathers and that fathers are included in services.

2

Fathers and UK Policy

Roger Olley and Carol Potter

Chapter Outline

Introduction

In this chapter, we will provide an overview of the current policy and legislative context in relation to fathers and what early years practitioners' obligations are within them in the UK. Key aspects of policies which focus on the importance of fathers as carers of their children will be highlighted, together with suggestions as to how agencies might begin to respond to them.

At the time of writing, the coalition government's policy in relation to fathers is still in the process of development, but early signs indicate a clear ongoing commitment to father inclusion. The coalition has not, to date, repealed any of the standing legislation or guidance and has stated its commitment to gender equality in the document *The Coalition: Our Programme for Government: Freedom, Fairness, Responsibility* (HM Government, 2010). These commitments include: reducing gender inequalities in the workplace; redressing the significant gender imbalance in the early years workforce; and promoting 'shared parenting' in early pregnancy. In addition, legislation in relation to paternity leave and the policy framework: *Supporting Families in the Foundation Years* (Department for

Education, 2011) all evidence a clear determination to support both mothers and fathers in their parenting roles.

Before discussing existing policy legislation in relation to fathers, we will begin by briefly reviewing the policy journey in relation to fathers during the last 30 years in order to contextualize the debate.

Fathers and policy: recent beginnings

Fathers began to be explicitly acknowledged in UK government policy towards the end of the 1980s, a trend observable in the USA and the EU. The reason for this was almost entirely based on economic concerns. For a number of reasons, there had been a significant increase in the number of lone-parent families. According to the National Statistics publication: Focus on Families (2005), one in four dependent children lived in a lone-parent family 2004, compared to 1 in 14 in 1972. Ninety percent of lone-parent families were headed by mothers, many of whom were dependent on state benefits. Successive Conservative government policies in the UK during this period were aimed at attempting to shift the financial cost of supporting lone-parent families from the state to individual fathers. Such attempts begin to be seen in the 1989 Children Act which permitted unmarried fathers to share parental responsibility by private agreement and more forcibly, the 1991 Child Support Act which required all fathers, married and divorced, to financially support biological children. The controversial Child Support Agency was established in 1993 to implement this legislation. In addition, successive UK governments have failed to address fundamental issues relating to work/family balance, a critical issue for UK fathers who have been found to work the longest hours in Europe. During the 1980s and 1990s, European directives regarding rights to extended parental leave at the birth of a child were rejected, again, a vital issue for fathering, since it is known, as outlined in Chapter 1, that early father involvement predicts later active participation. Little or no policy during this period focused on the importance of fathers as carers of their children, rather, policy attempted to address issues such as absent fathers and social order.

Lewis (2002) summarized UK policy towards fathers in the 1980–90s as driven, not by enabling practices to enhance father participation, but by negative perceptions that:

> they are increasingly unwilling to maintain their families and by the allied concern about the anti-social behaviour of young men who are not tied into families (p. 147).

New Labour: new approach

A significant change in government policy in relation to fathers gradually emerged under the New Labour government (1997–2010), as policy-makers began to take account of research demonstrating the beneficial impact of positive father involvement on child outcomes, as discussed in Chapter 1. Increasingly, the focus began to shift from the role of fathers as breadwinners towards the need for services to support men in their caring role. This change is apparent early in the New Labour administration, for example the 1998 Green Paper 'Supporting Families' (Home Office, 1998) stated: 'Fathers have a crucial role to play in their children's upbringing' (p. 50) and 'Early years services should be better co-ordinated and integrated to address complex individual needs; and involve parents (including fathers)' (p.14). Central to this change was an increasingly specific reference to 'fathers' as opposed to 'parents' in policy frameworks. Beverley Hughes, Minister of State for Children, summarized this position:

> Too often, when we talk about engaging parents, we actually only engage mothers. The automatic default position is that parent equals mother. This has to change. (The *Sunday Times*, 19 November 2006.)

New Labour introduced legislation to support the father's caring role. The 2003 Employment Act introduced two weeks' paid paternity leave for the first time. It is an indicator of government's acknowledgement of the importance of fathers that, in April 2011 legislation was amended to allow fathers to be able to take up to 26 weeks' extra paternity leave, in addition to their current entitlement of two weeks' statutory paternity leave.

New Labour went on to highlight the need for services to engage fathers in a number of key policy frameworks, which are examined below.

Fathers and policy: what it means for practice

At present, there are 28 key government policy and legislative documents which explicitly refer to fathers and/or father engagement in family support, health and education services. A full list of these is provided at the end of the book in Appendix 1, with examples of some key frameworks detailed below:

1 The Children Act (1989, 2004)
2 The National Service Framework for Children, Young People and Maternity Services: Core Standards (DH/DfES, 2004)

3 Engaging Fathers: Involving Parents, Raising Achievement (DfES, 2004)
4 The Equality Act (2006)
5 Sure Start Children's Centres: Practice Guidance; (DfES, 2006, 2007)
6 Gender Equality Duty and Local Government: Guidance for Public Authorities in England; (Equal Opportunities Commission (EOC), 2007)
7 Every Parent Matters (DfES, 2007)
8 The Children's Plan (DCSF, 2007)
9 The Healthy Child Programme (DH, Update 2009)
10 Maternity and Early Years: making a good start to family life (DH, DCSF, 2010)
11 Supporting Families in the Foundation Years (DH, 2011)

Examples of how current policy and strategy documents require or recommend the inclusion of fathers and father figures in services include:

The Framework for the Assessment of Children in Need and their Families (DH, 2000):

> requires assessors to take all resonable steps to gather information about, and from, all relevant family members, whether resident or not, and also requires them to be clear about the roles played by fathers or father figures

It continues in paragraph 2.12:

> The parenting tasks undertaken by fathers or father figures should be addressed alongside those of mothers or mother figures (p. 20)

Every Parent Matters (DfES, 2007) states that:

> Irrespective of the degree of involvement they have in the care of their children, fathers should be offered routinely the support and opportunities they need to play their parental role effectively (p. 10)

The Healthy Child Programme (HCP): *Pregnancy and the First Five Years of Life* (DH, 2009) requires that:

> Fathers should be routinely invited to participate in child health reviews, and should have their needs assessed (p. 11)

It also requires moving the HCP from:

> A focus mainly on mothers and children to working routinely with both mothers and fathers (whether they are living together or not (p. 15)

The Sure Start Children's Centres: Practice Guidance and *Planning and Performance Management Guidance* (DfES, 2006–2007) declares on page

20 that 'Involving fathers is crucial' and the *Sure Start Children's Centres: Performance, Achievements and Outcomes Review* (DfES, 2010) requires that all centres present information and evidence regarding how many fathers/ male carers have been involved in helping to plan services; what proportion of fathers have accessed services; whether the centre provides any activities targeted at fathers, or fathers from excluded or disadvantaged groups and what proportion of these fathers have accessed services.

Supporting Families in the Foundation Years (2010): this government guidance places fathers firmly at the centre of their children's early development, stating:

> From pregnancy onwards all professionals should consider the needs and perspectives of both parents. Government and the sector have a role to play in setting the right tone and expectation and helping professionals to think about how better to engage fathers in all aspects of their child's development and decisions affecting their child (p. 37).

One of the most important cross-cutting frameworks with major implications for service delivery to both men and women is The Gender Equality Duty which came into force on 6 April 2007 and which applies to all public authorities in England, Scotland and Wales. This duty supports and requires a shift towards an approach which recognizes differences between men and women and obliges services to deliver services in ways which are accessible to both, that is, providers are required to take a gender-differentiated approach to service delivery, of which more in Chapter 4. The Gender Equality Duty places a legal requirement on all public authorities and all private and voluntary organizations carrying out public functions, which includes policy-making, service delivery, employment, statutory discretion, and decision-making, to have due regard to the need to eliminate unlawful discrimination and harassment on the grounds of sex, and to promote equality of opportunity between women and men.

For our purposes, one of the most helpful changes in the development of policy language in the frameworks described above, is the increased use of the phrase 'mothers and fathers', in preference to the generic term 'parents' which has mostly been taken to mean mothers. Such language makes fathers much more visible to both policy-makers and practitioners.

Key issue for reflection

- The promotion of equal opportunities between women and men requires recognition that men and women are different in a number of significant ways. Do you agree with this statement and how might it affect your service?

For the practitioner, this large number of policy, strategy and guidance documents can seem to be overwhelming and confusing. It is important to recognize that the demands regarding father inclusion cannot be met unless the senior management team or senior manager of your agency, organization or team have put in place the infrastructure and the resources to allow it to happen. It is our experience that when father work in early years' settings does take place, it is usually developed and driven by a 'grassroots' worker or manager who has developed a particular interest in doing so. The work is not, on the whole, a result of a senior management team developing a carefully planned, financially supported, strategically constructed activity that meets the policy and strategic requirements placed upon them. The consequences of this 'grassroots' approach is that exciting, innovative and effective ways of engaging fathers may be developed but, because the work is outside of strategic and financial planning, a series of inevitable issues is likely to arise, such as:

- An incoherent management approach to father inclusion leads to an incoherent and ineffective staff team approach.
- Policy and strategic targets are not met effectively.
- Effective models of working are not shared across agencies and organizations.
- When the 'grassroots' individual worker or manager leaves, the work stops or becomes less effective.

For effective, sustainable early years working with fathers to take place, the senior management team need to identify and prioritize the policy and accountability requirements they wish to meet and then support the staff teams in attaining them.

Key issues for reflection

- What local strategies and policies are in place to inform and support your work with fathers?
- How might the development of specific policies and strategies help you in your work regarding father engagement?

Translating policy to practice: developing a position statement

One effective way of clarifying and supporting your agency's work with fathers, is to develop a position statement or policy statement that the team or workforce can work to. The value of developing such a document is significant in that it can inform and support work currently being delivered and inform and support all planned future working involving fathers and families.

It is important that agencies and the teams that work within them, have clarity of vision and clarity of purpose when trying to include fathers in their work. If services understand what it is they are trying to do, why they are trying to do it and what the principles behind the work are, then they are much more likely to be successful.

The key purpose of a position statement is that it gives managers, practitioners, service users and partner agencies a clear understanding of the provider's approach to working with fathers and male carers. Below you will find two different examples of possible position statements ranging from the simple and concise to the complex and demanding.

A simple position statement for early years' services could be:

> Children's Services in (enter locality) will commit to providing equality of service to male and female service users. Services recognize and respect the diversity and difference between male and female users and are committed to developing services, practices and employment opportunities which are responsive to their differing needs.

A local authority in the north-west of England is currently developing their position statement on involving fathers and male carers. They are moving from the very simple, but effective statement above, to a more complex form. Their draft statement reads:

> As an organization we believe: that all family members are of equal importance. Dads/family men make a difference as they play an essential role in children's lives. We will value the contribution that dads/family men make and endeavour to increase fathers' engagement with their children.
> We will demonstrate this position statement is being addressed by:
> - promoting awareness of the positive influence men have on child development
> - continued consultation with fathers and families
> - training staff to understand that engaging and working with fathers is not just one person's role but everybody's job

- training staff to give them the knowledge, skills and confidence to effectively engage with and work with fathers
- giving fathers equal access to resources – e.g. evening/weekend activities/ fathers-inclusive services
- developing a multi-agency approach with shared training opportunities
- requiring all commissioned services to demonstrate how they are meeting the requirements of the position statement.

This local authority continues to review, refine and develop their position statement but once it is agreed and finalized, they will have clarity of approach that will enable and support all staff to work with and include fathers in service provision. A key element of this statement is that they will be 'requiring all commissioned services to demonstrate how they are meeting the requirements of the position statement'. This is important because it ensures that all those providers who wish to undertake commissioned work for them have to indicate in their bid how they will include fathers in their work and how they will be evidencing this inclusion.

Key issues for reflection

- Does your agency have a position statement regarding father/male carer inclusion?
- If not, how could you develop such a statement?

It is critical to note that having a position statement and ensuring that it is implemented in practice are two different things. Making a position statement work requires time and effort to monitor that the requirements of the statement are met. A number of discrete processes will need to be put into place at each stage of service delivery to ensure that those aims enshrined within the position statement are achieved in practice and a wide range of strategies and approaches will be discussed at length in the following pages. For example, Chapter 3 explores the importance of collecting information on fathers as a first step to including them. Later chapters discuss the benefits of appointing fathers champions in each service to be responsible for driving forward father inclusion, and of appointing designated fathers' workers to develop the work within an overall whole-team framework where it is everyone's responsibility to include men. Finally, a number of specific strategies for engaging fathers at the level of everyday practice will be reviewed in detail.

Conclusion

We have shown that there is a wide range of both policy and legislative drivers which require service providers across all sectors to include fathers within their services. It is important to state, however, that the guidance and strategies outlined in this chapter are not just about meeting targets or ticking boxes. They are about effective working to improve outcomes for fathers, mothers and most importantly, children. There has been a significant shift in policy over recent years where the recognition of father involvement in families has moved from that of just 'provider' to one of being significant and important in the nurturing and caring of children. The *Think Family Service* toolkit (guidance note 2) (DCSF, 2010) states:

> While not all fathers and father-figures are able to be positively involved with their children, every effort should be made to support as many fathers as possible: all fathers, including those who may present certain risks, should have access to the information and support. Many children's services are still predominantly mother-focused and negative assumptions are often made that fathers are more interested in work than parenting or can't cope with children without a woman to help them. Ironically, these assumptions often lead to a situation where too much is expected of mothers (p. 15).

The importance of fathers in their children's lives has been recognized in research and this importance is now reflected in the policies and strategies which agencies and organizations are being asked to work to. It is essential that all workers, managers and leaders within agencies have an understanding of what these strategies and policies require and also what part they play in meeting those requirements.

Senior managers need to identify which of the many policies and strategies in place are a priority for their agency. They then need to make these priorities clear to their management teams. Management teams then need to inform grassroot workers what the priorities are and support them in meeting those priorities in their day-to-day working. If a service does not have clarity of purpose, clarity of vision and the planning and resources to meet their vision and purpose then it will not be achieved. This can only be to the detriment of the children they are seeking to serve. Engaging and working with fathers is the responsibility of each and every member of a team or organization. Policies and strategies, when fully implemented, can play a major part in supporting effective working with fathers and male carers.

3

Collecting Information: The First Step to Father Inclusion

David van der Velde and Charlotte Dack

Chapter Outline

> If we don't know who fathers are and where they are, then developing working relationships with fathers to support their children is not going to happen.
>
> [Early Years Practitioner]

Introduction

We would argue that collecting information on fathers is the single most important thing that services can do to begin the process of engaging large numbers of fathers. Failing to gather or use information that has been collected about fathers contributes significantly to father exclusion from services. If services do not know who fathers are, how can they offer or deliver support to them? This chapter will explore issues relating to the importance of gathering and using contact information for fathers and father figures in family and education services, with a specific focus on the early years. For a number of reasons, this key information is often not collected, despite policy requirements that it should be. The reasons for this and the implications of not collecting such information will be explored in detail.

This chapter will then go on to examine key issues in developing and managing father-inclusive information systems across a range of family and education services in the early years and beyond, providing case-study material to illustrate how such systems can be introduced, developed and made good use of.

As we saw in Chapter 1, positive father involvement in children's lives leads to better child outcomes in a number of areas. At the same time, services that do not capture information about fathers are failing to assess and manage risk factors in the minority of cases where this is a concern.

Collecting information on fathers: why is it so important?

The way in which services capture, store and process information about fathers and male carers often goes a long way to determining the extent to which fathers will be supported by services in future. As a general rule, the earlier in a child's life that services can engage with fathers and begin the process of relationship building, the more accessible they will be to fathers in the future. Collecting information on fathers/father figures is therefore the very first step on the road to father inclusion in services. If issues arise further down the line that might impact on the child's relationship with the father or male carer, such as relationship breakdown, or problems with physical or mental health in the family, it is far more likely that a father will turn to a practitioners for help if a relationship has already been established with a service. It is more difficult to begin the process of capturing information and communicating with fathers once problems have developed or when men have become disengaged from the family.

Services that capture information and begin the process of relationship building early in the fatherhood journey are far more likely to be successful in supporting fathers through difficulties, maximizing the benefit to the child from the father as a 'parenting resource'.

The early months: a golden opportunity

The antenatal period is a prime opportunity to begin the process of engaging positively with 'fathers-to-be' who are excited about the prospect of fatherhood and around 86% (Kiernan and Smith, 2003) of fathers in the UK are present at the birth. Where midwifery and health-visiting services work collaboratively and share information with early years services, the latter have been much more successful at capturing fathers' information, creating opportunities for early years staff to engage with fathers in general and to ensure that fathers are included in targeted service provision. To this end, it is important that there is a clear multi-disciplinary approach to father engagement across services.

On the other hand, where fathers' information is not captured early, services tend to be reliant on mothers to provide that information, thus mothers become the gatekeepers to fathers. Where there has been relationship breakdown between the parents, some mothers are reluctant for the father to be involved in the child's life. In some cases this may be for legitimate safety concerns (where the father represents a danger to mother or child) but in many cases this may be because the parents have struggled to separate difficulties in their own relationship with each other from the relationship that each of them has with their child.

Invisible men: what are the consequences?

Where services miss opportunities to collect information about fathers and male carers, the fathers may become 'invisible' to services. There may be a father with unmet support needs involved in the child's life but services do not know who or where he is or have any means of engaging with him and not meeting fathers' needs in such circumstances may have a range of negative consequences for children, fathers and mothers. At the same time, neither will fathers know about what help is available to them. When men are invisible to services, they are also denied the opportunity to participate in service development and this can lead to an increasing gap between the needs of fathers in a community and the support services that are available.

> **Key issues for reflection**
>
> - Does your service routinely collect information on fathers/father figures?
> - What sort of information do you collect?
> - Where are the gaps?

We hope to have demonstrated the crucial importance of ensuring that information on fathers is routinely collected. To some extent, the need for such father-inclusive data-collection systems have been recognized at government level in the UK, as we shall explore in the next section.

What does government policy and guidance say?

Recent government policies and guidance have placed obligations on services to be gender differentiated in the way they deliver services. As we saw in the previous chapter, a gender-differentiated approach requires services to recognize and respond to the different needs of male and female service users. For example, a martial-arts-based health improvement programme is likely to be more attractive to men than arts and crafts sessions.

The following legislation and policy frameworks are just a few of those which require services to work with fathers. In all cases, the very first requirement for agencies in delivering services to fathers is that they know who the men are and have a means of contacting them:

- The Gender Duty in the Equality Act of 2006, which, as we saw in Chapter 2, places a statutory duty on public services to meet the different needs of men and women.
- Aiming High for Children: Supporting Families from HM Treasury and Department for Education and Skills (2007) which specifies that midwives and health visitors have a role in supporting *both* parents.
- The Sure Start Children's Centres: Planning and Performance Management Guidance from the Department for Education and Skills (2006–2007) requires children's centres to have effective systems to gather information about fathers in all the families they are in contact with.

In universal services, these directives ought to mean that information management systems are father inclusive, that information is gathered routinely about fathers and male carers of the child and that correspondence is sent out to both male and female carers. Sadly, in the extensive experience of Fathers Plus, an organization which has worked in the field of father inclusion for over a decade, this is still rarely the case.

Where other agencies, such as those listed above, do engage with fathers, it is common for them to be blind to the parental responsibilities of the men they work with. For example, a man who separates from the mother of his child and looks to his local housing department to be rehoused, may well be offered accommodation that does not facilitate him being able to continue overnight contact with his child.

It is clear then, that there are a number of drivers at policy level in favour of gathering information on fathers/father figures across a range of services. In the next section, we will explore the extent to which services have been successful in complying with such guidance, discussing possible reasons for omissions.

Data-collection systems: what do services know about fathers?

In universal family services, the focus is generally on the mother and child. In 2003, a report on father involvement in Sure Start found that 'systematic standardized data on father participation in Sure Start activities across programmes were not available' because programmes were not collecting that information (p. 28). For this reason, it was hard for researchers to reach firm conclusions regarding the level of father involvement in services. Targeted social care services are now beginning to implement standard procedures to gather information about the men involved in the lives of children deemed to be at risk. Despite this, there remain numerous issues within a range of services with the routine capture and processing information about these men who can have such a significant influence on children's lives.

Maternity services and health visiting

Maternity and health-visiting services tend to be focused on the needs of the mother and the child. The document 'Towards Better Births' (Commission for Healthcare Audit and Inspection, 2008) which reported on a major review of maternity services in the UK mentioned fathers only once and mothers over 130 times. With over 80% of fathers now attending the birth of their child, these services have a golden opportunity to begin developing a positive relationship with fathers, supporting their needs and helping them to bond with their new baby at this crucial time. In reality, information about fathers can be limited to identifying a limited range of factors which may include, for example, any indicators of domestic violence.

A major culture shift is needed within health and maternity services to reach a point where information about fathers' as well as mothers' needs is identified and responded to from the early stages of pregnancy. It is still relatively rare for maternity services to provide any information targeted specifically at fathers and many practitioners may still not view this as an important aspect of their role. The Fatherhood Institute has produced an important publication: 'Including New Fathers: A Guide to Maternity Professionals' in which they emphasize the need to register fathers' details, so that services can begin to provide support to men.

Post-natal visits from health visitors represent a great opportunity to capture information about male family members that could be shared with early years services such as Sure Start. The extent to which information is gathered about men tends to be dependent on the attitude of the individual health visitor and concerns over information sharing from health services make it very difficult to identify the extent to which this does take place.

Sure Start children centres and nurseries

In the earliest days of the Sure Start programme, some systems, however unwittingly, excluded fathers and male carers altogether, with registration forms and databases asking only for information about child and 'parent'. As the research evidence adding weight to the case for including fathers was followed by a series of new government policies and guidance, systems were amended or redeveloped to 'include fathers'.

To date however, there remains a significant gender imbalance in the registration of parents within children's centres. Based on the experience of the Fathers Plus service working with a number of UK local authorities, it is estimated that no more than 25% of children have the father's information included in their registration.

Schools

It is now widely accepted that the quality of parenting is one of the most significant determinants of a child's progress and achievement at school (Desforges and Abouchaar, 2003). As such, parental engagement is a key plank of the Ofsted inspection framework for schools. The 2009 Evaluation Schedule requires inspectors to take account of the effectiveness with which the school communicates with all parents and carers with parental responsibility, including those who may be reluctant or unsure about approaching the school, such as mothers and fathers not living with their children.

At present, it often remains the exception rather than the rule for schools to send out separate communications to fathers and mothers. It is usually largely mothers who attend meetings at school regarding additional support or behaviour issues and many men report feeling uncomfortable in primary schools staffed predominantly by women (Page et al., 2008).

As such, mothers often remain the gatekeepers to the father's involvement in their child's learning in school. Most schools now require 'parents' (usually mothers) to complete home–school agreements around supporting their child's learning. This could be a good opportunity for schools to begin developing relationships with fathers by utilizing home–school agreements that require separate information from the father or second carer of the child.

The following section discusses a range of factors which can prevent services capturing and processing information about fathers and male carers effectively. Approaches to overcoming such barriers are also provided.

Father-inclusive information systems: barriers and ways forward

There are a range of barriers to the development of father-inclusive information systems, principal among which are concerns about data protection, mothers as gatekeepers and general lack of awareness as to the importance of collecting information on fathers/father figures.

Data-protection concerns

Most local authorities are reluctant to allow services to capture and process information about fathers and male carers without the written consent of the father himself. Locally, guidance on this issue tends to come from legal services' departments whose concerns over data-protection requirements often lead them to take a 'risk averse' stance.

As such, some services will only register the father's details if he is present, while others post out registration forms in the hope that fathers will complete and return them. This practice tends to exclude those fathers least amenable to engaging with services, who are, in general, the ones most likely to be in need of the support the service can offer.

These data-protection concerns are unfounded. Fathers Plus and The Fatherhood Institute are often asked about the legality of collecting information on fathers in their absence. Both organizations checked the legality of doing so with (1) Department for Education lawyers (2) Department of Health lawyers; and (3) The Information Commissioner's Office (the UK's independent authority set up to promote access to official information and to protect personal information). These authorities on the subject advised that it is legal to collect contact details for fathers when they are not present, provided that certain procedures are adhered to; these are detailed later in this chapter under 'Quick guide to developing father-inclusive information systems'. In addition, guidance from the Department for Children, Schools and Families stated that The Data Protection Act allows you to gather the details on any person who is considered important to a child's well-being (such as a father) from a 'third party', such as the mother. Within health services, the protection of patient information is covered by the Caldicott guidelines.

Ways forward

Services from local authorities and other agencies should ensure that up-to-date advice about data protection is adopted in the development of registration procedures.

Key issues for reflection

- What is the guidance you have on information sharing between agencies?
- Does this mention the issue of father's information and is it based on the latest government guidance, detailed above?

Mothers as gatekeepers

As it is generally mothers who first register with services, they are often the only potential source of information for practitioners about the child's father or male carer. Macleod (2000) suggested that many women may 'unconsciously operate within the norm of male un-involvement', not necessarily viewing limited father involvement in aspects of their child's life as problematic (Goldman, 2005). Some mothers may be reluctant to involve the father for other reasons, including beliefs that fathers do not need to be directly involved due to legitimate concerns about safety (in the case of domestic violence or abuse) or simply due to the difficult feelings that persist after the breakdown of the relationship between the mother and father.

Whatever the reason, without contact information for fathers/male carers, services cannot engage with the father to identify potential risks or support positive co-parenting (see Chapter 10 for more information on issues of separated fathers). Again, it is the fathers of children most at risk or in need of support who are likely to be excluded as a result of this situation.

This issue is a difficult one to address, given not only the safety concerns, but also the reluctance of practitioners to jeopardize their working relationship with the mother by insisting on gathering fathers' details.

Ways forward

Appropriate training and guidance for practitioners should improve the extent to which they can safely and constructively work with mothers to engage fathers.

Key issues for reflection

- Do your staff feel confident about articulating to mothers, fathers and colleagues, why it is important to include fathers wherever possible in order to improve outcomes for children?
- How could your service improve their confidence in this area?

Ensuring effective use of father information

Registering information about fathers and male carers is far from being the end of the story when it comes to delivering inclusive services. *Developing systems to capture the father's contact details does not mean that fathers will be kept informed and included in processes unless the protocols and systems are also gender differentiated.* For example, in universal services, children's centres now include a space on their registration forms for the father or second carer's details, but it seems that such information is often not well used for keeping fathers informed and for gathering ongoing information from fathers about their child's development. In one local authority a great deal of resources had gone into registering the details of resident and non-resident fathers and male carers and this led to a significant increase in the proportion of male parents on the Sure Start database. However, any letters that were sent out still only went to the identified 'main carer' and it transpired that the 'main carer' was identified on the database by the admin. staff who processed the registration forms. The admin. staff had not had any training in working with fathers and their default assumption was that mother was the main carer. Thus despite the investment in capturing father's contact details, fathers were still reliant on mothers to gain access to information and services.

In social care settings, most services now routinely gather information about the identities of male members of the family for a child in need. However, in processes such as the Common Assessment Framework (CAF) and the Team around the Family (TAF), the extent to which fathers and male carers are included in meetings and procedures varies greatly between services and again often comes down to the attitude of the individual practitioner.

Ways forward

In order to address this issue, it is essential for all services to review their protocols and procedures to ensure they use information collected on fathers by providing opportunities to include fathers on each occasion they exchange information with the family.

Information on attendance: is it gender differentiated?

Collecting registration information on fathers represents only the start of the journey towards father inclusion. Fathers must then be offered information about services, be proactively recruited and supported in their ongoing use of services, processes which are discussed elsewhere, in detail, in this book. At each stage, it is essential to have data-collection systems in place to monitor the extent to which fathers/male carers are actually using services. As stated above in 2003, a report on father involvement in Sure Start found that that 'systematic standardized data on father participation in Sure Start activities across programmes were not available' (p. 28) because programmes were not collecting that information. For this reason, it was hard for researchers to reach firm conclusions regarding the level of father involvement in services.

Ways forward

It is important for services to have recording systems which enable them to monitor how many fathers are registered with their service, how many have been offered information and how many are actually using services. A good starting point is to routinely monitor and review the gender breakdown of registration and attendances at different kinds of service provision. This would enable managers to identify providers who perform better at including fathers leading to the sharing of good practice between services.

Key issues for reflection

Can you access information about the proportion of fathers/mothers:
- registered with your service?
- receiving information?
- attending universal services?
- attending TAF/TAC meetings? contributing to CAFs?
- Are variations in these figures between services/settings/lead practitioners attributable to different approaches?
- Is there good practice in one area that could be disseminated?

Below, we provide a quick guide to developing father-inclusive information systems.

Quick guide to developing father-inclusive information systems

Below, we summarize the steps involved in collecting registration information on fathers/father figures.

Collecting father information: making the case

In most cases, children are registered at nurseries, schools and children's centres by the mother. It is important that the staff involved in the registration process have appropriate training, are aware of the corporate policy and can explain to mothers why involvement of fathers and male carers is important to their children, although in some cases mothers may not have or may refuse to give contact details for the father, for very valid reasons.

Father-friendly fact sheets

Services should have father/male-carer-specific information such as Father Fact Sheets and Men-friendly communications on a range of issues, such as breastfeeding and the importance of play, for example.

Contacting fathers after collecting information

Where information about the father (or another carer) is supplied by the mother/carer in his absence, you should ask the mother to let the father know that they have given this information. In addition, once you, as an agency, have registered information about the father or other carer in their absence, it is important that you let them know as soon as possible what details you hold about them. A system should be in place to ensure that a worker will phone the father as soon as possible to explain how it is that you have their details (for example – they were supplied by the child's mother) and why you want to hold information about parents/carers. It is also very important this call should also be used to tell fathers what your agency does and what you can offer fathers and male carers.

Who else can access the data?

You should tell parents about any other agencies that could access the information you hold about them and in what circumstances, emphasizing the possible benefits for children and families. For example, do you share registration information with social services, schools, maternity services and so on?

Removing or changing information

You should provide a simple way for parents to contact you to change or remove their information on your records (for example a tear-off reply sheet on a written form or phone number). You should have systems in place to make sure that records are changed/deleted as requested.

Productive use of father information

You should then have a clear set of guidelines for the ongoing use of father information and an accountability structure to ensure that this information is used productively to keep fathers informed and engaged over time.

Recording all father engagement

You need to record the engagement of both fathers and mothers with services (attendances etc.) and should be able to access this information easily to determine to what extent your service is including men in practice.

Below, we provide a case study in which these guidelines were put into practice in a father-involvement project in Sunderland. In this project, registration data was used in conjunction with a database recording fathers' attendances at a range of parenting support activities. Such a complex and sophisticated system provides an example of what can be achieved when father-inclusive systems are developed from the ground up.

My Dad Matters Programme in Sunderland

When in 2010, the Sunderland Family and Parenting team set about addressing the gender imbalance in the take-up of the parenting offer by fathers and male carers, they worked in partnership with Children North East, Fathers Plus to develop a new service from the ground up.

The new programme 'My Dad Matters in Sunderland' aimed to engage men with no previous involvement with services and support them to improve their parenting.

Before the programme began in Sunderland, only 8% of parents/ carers who attended their Universal Parenting Offer were male. After the first four months of delivery, over 150 men had been enrolled on the programme and by August 2010, 63% of the parents/carers who accessed a parenting service in Sunderland were male.

Designing information systems from scratch to enable work with fathers was the opposite of what usually happens in family services where systems that have been designed and developed from a 'parent means mother' perspective have had 'father' or ' second carer' details bolted on.

The enrolment form that was adopted requested not only standard contact information but also age details for the 'family men' and the child(ren) as well as details about men's family situation, such as whether they live with the child, whether they are a father, stepfather, grandfather etc. Such questions can be sensitive and it is therefore essential to make it clear that such information is being asked for in order to help services design and deliver better services for families and children. For example, different kinds of provision may be required by non-resident as opposed to resident fathers.

The enrolment form is designed to work with the Fathers Plus service-user database, which holds the enrolment information about the men and enables this to be cross-referenced against parenting sessions accessed and also against the feedback from participants in the form of entry and exit questionnaires.

Capturing data in this way about family men and their involvement in services means that it is possible to identify not only which programmes and services are being accessed by men in different family circumstances, but also the quality of the interventions (based on service-user feedback). For example, it might be found that a '"Dad to Be" programme' is attracting more resident than non-resident fathers.

Conclusion

Father involvement has been shown to lead to better outcomes for children and families but at present most support for the parenting role continues to be offered and delivered to mothers. The first step to changing this situation is to routinely collect information on fathers in every agency setting so that services can be regularly offered to men. The next step is to record service use by fathers, as distinct from mothers so that it is possible to determine how effective your service is in including men over time. The collection of data on service use by 'parents' will not provide this information and is therefore likely to perpetuate the ongoing under-representation of men in family services.

Summary of chapter

- Information about fathers is important for services that wish to help fathers support children and families.
- Services need to capture information early in the fatherhood journey rather than when difficulties may have begun to arise within families.
- Protocols for capturing and sharing information need to be agreed across services especially between maternity services and early years.
- Most importantly: services should record and monitor mothers and fathers separately in all your activity. Identify and learn from what works well.

Part 2
Fathers in Early Years Services

4

Engaging Fathers in the Antenatal and Post-natal Periods

Roger Olley

Chapter Outline

Introduction

In this chapter, the importance of including fathers in the antenatal and post-natal periods will be discussed, together with approaches to working successfully with fathers at these early stages. Barriers to and practical strategies for engaging with this specific group of fathers will be considered, drawing upon both the academic literature and case study material from practitioners.

It is important that practitioners and professionals who are reading this chapter do so with a questioning mind. A series of reflective questions are interspersed throughout this chapter and I urge readers to stop and reflect upon the 'Key issues for reflection' as they arise.

The importance of including fathers in the antenatal/post-natal periods

Stephen Bavolek (1990) in his paper 'The Art and Science of Raising Healthy Children' states:

> parenting is a practice as old as human life itself, is considered by many to be the singular most important form of human interaction. ...it is generally agreed that the impact of parenting is felt throughout one's lifetime – and for succeeding generations. No other form of human interaction can boast such power and longevity (p. 1).

Fathers need as much information and support as possible to enable them to undertake this 'singular most important form of human interaction' to the best of their abilities. Research indicates that fathers are important for families, and that they have a significant impact on outcomes for children. Maternity and early years services have traditionally focused on the needs of the mother during pregnancy, birth and early childhood but as we saw in Chapter 2, there is a recognition and a demand in government policies and strategies that agencies need to pay closer attention to including fathers in their work.

The *National Service Framework for Children, Young People and Maternity Services* was published by the Department of Health in autumn 2004. It is a ten-year programme intended to stimulate long-term and sustained improvement in children's health. It states that:

> the role of fathers in parenting their children is frequently overlooked. Their contribution to their child's development and well-being is important. Good parenting by fathers can significantly promote their child's development.' it recognizes the significance of fathers in influencing their children's lives in a positive way and 'supports a cultural shift in all service provision, to include fathers in all aspects of a child's well-being (Standard 2. Paragraph 3.6).

This is a clear statement, in a significant strategy document, on the importance of fathers in children's lives and on the importance of engaging them in services. It acknowledges that services are not yet adequately engaging fathers in the services they provide. Difficulty of working success-fully with fathers was again highlighted in 2009 by the Department of Health (DH) in the *Healthy Child Programme* (HCP): *Pregnancy and the First Five Years of Life.*

This programme is described by the DH as the early intervention and prevention public health programme that *'lies at the heart'* of all universal services for children and families and it is seen as *'a best practice guide for children's services'*. It explicitly recognizes the importance of fathers in terms of outcomes in children's lives.

Page 11 of the HCP emphasizes the vital contribution that fathers make to their children's development, health and well-being, and notes that often services do not sufficiently recognize or support them, despite wide-ranging evidence demonstrating that a father's behaviour, beliefs and aspirations can profoundly influence the health and well-being of both mother and child in both positive and negative ways.

Fathers and breastfeeding

An example of how giving fathers information can lead to positive outcomes is shown in a small-scale study conducted by Wolfberg et al. (2004). This study tested the effectiveness of a simple educational intervention for fathers-to-be that was designed to encourage fathers to advocate for breast-feeding and to assist their partner if she chose to breastfeed. Researchers undertook a randomized controlled trial in which 59 fathers-to-be were randomly assigned to attend either a 2-hour intervention class on infant care and breastfeeding promotion (intervention) or a class on infant care only (control group). They found that overall, breastfeeding was initiated by 74% of women whose partners attended the intervention class, as compared with 41% of women whose partners attended the control class and they concluded that:

> expectant fathers can be influential advocates for breastfeeding, playing a critical role in encouraging a woman to breastfeed her newborn infant.

Singh and Newburn (2003) assert that as fathers are a source of support for women, they should be provided with information and support themselves in order to be able to fulfil this role.

The case to include fathers in antenatal/post-natal services is a strong one. Fathers matter, for good or ill, to outcomes for children and if practitioners do not include fathers in their work then they are failing to make best use of the resources available to them and consequently may fail the children they seek to serve.

Key issues for reflection

- Do you and your colleagues fully appreciate *why* it is important to include fathers in the antenatal/post-natal periods?
- Does your service provision include fathers in '*all aspects of a child's well being*'?
- Is your team aware of its responsibilities regarding father inclusion in terms of national policies and guidance?

Barriers to including fathers in antenatal/post-natal services

Despite the many benefits to be accrued from including fathers in the very early stages of their children's lives, there are a number of barriers to including men in antenatal/post-natal services and the most important of these are explored below.

Mother-focused working

The 2009 'Think Family Toolkit' notes in paragraph 44 that:

> Many children's services are still predominantly mother-focused and negative assumptions are often made that fathers are more interested in work than parenting (p. 15, para. 44).

The Healthy Child Programme (2009) observes that both maternity and child health services are much more used to working with mothers, and this has an effect on their ability to engage with fathers. Antenatal and post-natal services are, on the whole highly feminized environments. The Nursing and Midwifery Council *Statistical analysis of the register 1 April 2006 to 31 March 2007* notes that there are 35,172 midwives of which only 134 are male and 24,530 health visitors of which only 371 are male. In addition, the Children's Workforce Development Council (in 2010) noted that the children's and young people's workforce consists largely of female workers (98%).

It is predominantly women who staff agencies which work in antenatal/post-natal and early years settings and, after the child, it is largely women who are seen as the main 'customers' of those services, since they are, of course, physically pregnant. Having said this, it is vital to acknowledge the fact that while the father is not physically pregnant, he is 'pregnant' emotionally, socially, financially and psychologically and the needs arising from these dispositions have to be addressed.

Key issues for reflection

- How do you respond to the notion of the 'pregnant man'?
- How might such a notion influence your view of service provision?

Personal attitudes and experience

Each and every practitioner working in early years systems holds an intensely personal experience of fathers, fathering and of men and it is possible that this personal view may impact, in a number of ways, on the way practitioners relate to and communicate with fathers. Men may be viewed by some practitioners as posing a potential risk to wives, partners or themselves. The Home Office (1999), *Domestic Violence: Findings from a new British Crime Survey self-completion questionnaire* found that one in four women had been subject to physical, emotional, sexual or economic abuse by a male partner. As the early years workforce is 98% female, it is possible that a quarter of the female staff members of agencies involved in antenatal and post-natal services may themselves have had negative experiences of men in their lives. It is not known if or how these experiences impact upon their professional ability to engage with and work with men but managers need to be aware of the possibility of personal experience clouding or affecting professional working and that there may be a need to provide support and counselling to their staff teams. It should be noted that if one in four of the workforce have experienced domestic violence then *that means that* three in four have not. It should also be noted settings such as clinics, Sure Start centres, drop-ins and playgroups can be 'safe havens' for women and staff who have negative experiences of men, as they will be confident that male participation in these settings is minimal or non-existent. It is important that the needs of these women are recognized and supported. However, professionals should take care that by meeting the needs of these groups they do not exclude fathers when doing so. It will be necessary to develop agreement among the predominantly female workforce, partner organizations and parent partners that working with men and fathers is in the majority of cases both desirable and safe. Working with fathers may be challenging, demanding and lengthy work but it is important that those seeking to develop effective working with fathers develop a researched base 'corporate view' of fathers, fathering and of what they are trying to achieve and why they are trying to achieve it. Teams and individual workers may need to be supported in disassociating their personal experience of fathering, fathers and men from professional practice. If you have a whole team who understand and who can collectively articulate, from a research basis, the importance of fathers and the consequences of poor or absent fathering for children, then success is more likely to occur.

Key issues for reflection

- Do you view fathers and men as a potential risk or a resource?
- How much do you think your personal experience might influence your professional practice?

Antenatal classes: how father inclusive?

One of the key strategies for supporting parents during pregnancy is the provision of antenatal classes. How effective are these in relation to fathers-to-be? Singh and Newburn (2000) undertook an antenatal postal survey of 817 UK men in which 57% of men replied to a follow-up questionnaire 3–5 months after the birth. This survey found high levels of dissatisfaction among the men, with one man in three wanting information on nineteen possible topics after their antenatal classes had finished. This study found that a significant number of men perceived antenatal education classes to be largely woman focused and that they did not sufficiently recognize or respond to their information and support needs. Finally, fathers felt that classes did not adequately recognize their important role as fathers-to-be. The survey also found that the men *did* want to be involved in their partners' antenatal/postnatal care and that they wanted to be given information about pregnancy and childbirth and their future lives with their new baby.

We will now move on to discuss strategies and approaches to including fathers in the very early stages of their children's lives.

Including fathers from the start: approaches

A cultural shift

The first major issue to raise is that organizations involved in the delivery of services in the antenatal and post-natal periods need to undergo a 'cultural shift' in the way they view fathers and the services they offer them at this crucial time. One of the most important cultural shifts required is that fathers-to-be and new fathers are not viewed and responded to as solely the partner and supporter of the pregnant woman and mother but rather viewed as being 'pregnant' as a father-to-be in their own right.

Obviously, as discussed above, the father is not physically pregnant but he is 'pregnant' emotionally, socially, financially and psychologically. If services are able to provide accessible, meaningful, timely information and support that meet the father's needs as a 'pregnant man' and as a new father then services will have prepared and supported an individual much more prepared and able for the *'singular most important form of human interaction'* that we call parenting.

The 'Think Family Toolkit' (DCSF, 2009) states:

> Making services more welcoming to fathers doesn't necessarily mean a drastic overhaul – small things can make a big difference. To engage successfully with fathers, it is important to take a systematic approach to understanding their needs and assessing services. There are many simple things that can be done immediately to reach out to fathers, such as making small changes to your environment and holding a staff focus group to share experiences of engaging with fathers (p. 15, para. 45).

A key point that practitioners should recognize is that the vast majority of fathers are loving, nurturing men who care deeply about their children and who are keen to ensure that their children get the best possible start in life. Being able to inform fathers how your service can help them ensure their children get the best possible start is key to engaging them in your work.

A gender-differentiated approach

Antenatal and post-natal services are now being offered from a variety of settings such as health centres, Sure Start children's centres and community and voluntary settings. It is important that fathers view these settings as being open, accessible and meaningful to them. In their study of family centres,

Ghate et al. (2000) identified three distinct approaches to working with mothers and fathers. These were:

- Agnostic – services have no identified approach to working with men (they have not thought about it)
- Gender neutral – services which regard men as the same as women, and offer the same services, courses and resources to women and men (they have made a conscious decision)
- Gender differentiated – services which regard men and women as having different needs which need to be addressed differently, requiring the provision of different experiences, courses and resources for men in order to attract them to the services and to maintain their engagement.

This book strongly advocates a gender-differentiated approach to working with fathers and male carers, as this is widely accepted as being the most effective way of attracting and maintaining father involvement. By adopting a GD approach, factors such as timing of events and activities, appropriateness of materials, resources and courses and accessibility of venues all come under scrutiny and are considered in terms of male use and acceptability. Policy-makers have recognized that gender-differentiated early years policy and practice, which requires services to be accessible to both fathers and mothers, will best harness the many attributes which both parents bring to family life.

Key issues for reflection

- Is your service gender agnostic, gender blind or gender differentiated in its approach to working with fathers and mothers?
- What evidence do you have to support your conclusion?

A whole-team approach

Another key issue to address, is that the successful engagement of fathers in the antenatal/post-natal periods is not just the business of any designated 'fathers worker'. Recruiting and engaging fathers requires a whole-team, whole-systems approach that involves all team members regardless of their role or responsibility. Administration, reception and front-of-house staff are crucial to the process. Administration teams are essential to registering the fathers as we saw in the previous chapter: if a team does not know who the fathers are and where the fathers are then they cannot include them in services. They are also essential to ensuring that the fathers receive timely and appropriate communications such as invites to sessions and activities. Reception and front-of-house staff will usually be the first point of contact for a father entering your service for the first time. If your reception staff have been trained to welcome fathers and give them appropriate information when required, you will find that the fathers are more likely to re-attend at a later date.

The Healthy Child Programme

Having discussed some of the more general issues associated with including fathers in ante and post-natal services, we shall now turn to some more specific issues and strategies as discussed in *The Healthy Child Programme* (HCP): *Pregnancy and the First Five Years of Life* (DH, 2009) which 'lies at the heart' of all universal services and is intended to act as a best practice guide for children's services (p. 6). It explicitly recognizes the importance of fathers in terms of outcomes in children's lives and makes clear how fathers should be engaged in service provision. The HCP places a major emphasis on parenting support and is very specific in terms of the input early years agencies should provide. On page 10, it lists a number of very specific issues to be addressed by agencies regarding fathers, namely:

- supporting fathers to provide sensitive and attuned parenting, in particular during the first months and years of life
- supporting strong couple relationships and stable positive relationships within families, in accordance with *The Children's Plan* (Department for Children, Schools and Families, 2007b)
- ensuring that contact with the family routinely involves and supports fathers, including non-resident fathers
- supporting the transition to parenthood, especially for first-time fathers.

The HCP also recognizes the importance of fathers for issues such as breastfeeding and maternal depression. It advises that agencies should pay due attention to:

> Providing information and advice to fathers, to encourage their support for breastfeeding (p. 35).

And on the issue of maternal depression, the HCP states that there should be post-natal parent–infant groups with enhanced components for fathers. It also suggests that sessions should address and respond to the specific concerns of fathers, including how to support their partner, caring for infants, and all of the emotional and psychological issues which arise from fatherhood.

To meet the HCP's ambitions will require all agencies, organizations and practitioners working in antenatal and post-natal services to develop new ways of service delivery that are father inclusive. The *Healthy Child Programme* (p. 26) contains good practice suggestions for engaging fathers in the ante- and post-natal periods:

- 'Make it explicit that the HCP is there for the whole family – including the father ... Address him directly, encourage him to speak and make it clear that you are listening.'
- 'Arrange meetings, services, groups and reviews to maximize the possibility of fathers attending. Stress the importance of their presence to both them and the mother.'
- 'Record fathers' details – including those of non-resident fathers. Most mothers will give this information willingly, and two in three pregnant women who are not living with the father of their child describe him as "a good friend" or as their partner.'
- 'Include an assessment of the father's needs as well as the mother's, as these will have a direct impact on both the mother and the child.'
- 'Include an assessment of the father's health behaviours (e.g. in relation to diet, smoking, and alcohol or drug use), asking him directly wherever possible. These behaviours have a direct impact on both the mother and the child, and specifically on the mother's own health behaviours.'
- 'Signpost fathers to all of the relevant services.'

Key issues for reflection

- Are you and your team aware of the demands of the Healthy Child Programme?
- Do you, as a team, have a strategy for meeting the demands of the programme?
- How can you evidence that you are meeting the demands of the programme?

In addition to the suggestions described in the Healthy Child Programme, we will now explore other important strategies for engaging men in the very early years.

Marketing services to fathers

You need to be able to understand what it is that you are offering to fathers or, to put it another way, what you are selling to them. If you have clarity about the product you are selling and the benefits that product will bring to the customer (the father) then you will be more likely to persuade him to take it up. Having clarity about what is 'in it for the dad and his child' will also allow you to develop advertising and resources to communicate the benefits of your service effectively.

Services should make a clear statement to fathers and male carers, by advertising, posters, letters and word of mouth that they actively want to work with fathers, that their service is for fathers and that the service has something to offer fathers. One way of doing this is to put the statement 'Sure Start is for dads too' or 'midwives/health visitors are for dads too', on any literature, letters, emails or advertising that you send out. Put posters up that state this simple fact clearly. Fathers do not, on the whole, understand that your service is available to them and that your service has something to offer them. Proactively seek out contact with 'antenatal dads' by engaging with the workers who have the highest level of contacts during this period, e.g. Midwives/Health Visitors/Practice Nurses. Ask them to deliver targeted letters/flyers and information sheets that are specifically targeted at dads-to-be and which invite them to use your services.

Use the 'golden moments' when fathers are present in large numbers. For example, contact fathers at the scan clinic to 'sell them' the services you offer. Significant numbers of fathers attend the first and second scans. Fathers' attendance at the birth of their child is now considered very much the norm; offer fathers information, resources and opportunities for continued involvement in services while they are at their most receptive.

Normalize father involvement: antenatal classes

It is important to 'normalize' fathers' involvement in service activities at the earliest opportunity. We suggest the antenatal period as a prime involvement time. It should be remembered that first-time parents, including first-time fathers, are typically unsure about their new 'parenting' role but are eager to learn and do their best for their new infant. Midwives, and those they work with, are usually the couple's first formal encounter with the world of 'parenting'. By not taking up the opportunity to *meaningfully* include fathers in antenatal discussion and classes, they may be receiving the message that they are viewed as secondary parents right from the start. It should be remembered that antenatal classes may be the only parent-education programme these fathers will attend and therefore their importance should not be underestimated. Furthermore, actively include fathers in any antenatal home-visiting plan. Often fathers may be unwittingly ignored or marginalized when home visits take place.

You might also consider offering a 'preparation for fatherhood' session which could be held in tandem with the antenatal classes and a 'Pre Dad' health check up that will give him the opportunity to resolve any questions he may have, but also to allow agencies to establish contact with him.

Collecting information

As was discussed above in Chapter 3, it is vital to ensure that the fathers' as well as the mothers' details are collected when registering families to your service. Whenever possible, separated or disengaged fathers' contact details should be acquired if possible, following sensitive discussions with the mother. If an agency does not have a father's contact details how can it contact and engage with fathers?

Including fathers in the post-natal period: approaches

Below we outline a number of approaches for retaining father involvement after the birth of their child.

- Consider offering services outside the usual 9 to 5 Monday to Friday systems.
- A significant number of fathers attend clinics to buy the 'baby milk'. Talk to them there or arrange for a questionnaire or letter, aimed just at them, to be given to them as they buy the milk. If the men are attending to buy 'baby milk', then offer them a service they will value at the same time, such as access to newspapers with local employment opportunities in them, a 'dads' news board' which informs them of local/children's-centre events they can access with their children or a 'job club' which they can join.
- Offer a series of short, focused activities that are relevant to the situation dads are in at a particular time – e.g. a weaning session when their child is 8 weeks old, a 'first aid' session a week after the birth or managing 'temper tantrums' at two years.
- Set up an activity-focused weekly 'drop in', such as 'Top Tots' or a 'Messy Play' session that can be used by mums with the specific and stated aim of their encouraging dads' participation.
- Put fathers as a regular item on the agenda at team meetings.
- Contact new post-natal fathers, send them a 'congratulations' card, which tells them that your service is for 'fathers too', include in it a list of activities available.
- Try not to think just in terms of having a 'dads' group' but think of normalizing dads' involvement in your service's opportunities and activities.
- Appoint a father's champion in your team whose job is to ask the question, 'What about the dads, how do they fit in?' whenever services, activities or resources are being developed or discussed.

Contacting fathers through mothers

It is possible that sometimes agencies and services will encounter some resistance to the inclusion of fathers and male carers into their services by a small number of mothers. This may be due to factors such as differing views of fathers and male carers' roles, domestic violence, territorialism or a concern that 'female' space is being entered. A clear, whole-team strategy should be developed and implemented which addresses these issues in a positive, cohesive and sensitive way.

Fathers can be reached through mothers by:

- asking mothers to deliver and return letters/invitations/questionnaires for fathers
- involving mothers in recruiting their partners to groups or activities
- consulting and engaging with fathers and fathers-to-be, who attend appointments with their partners
- delivering, through their partners if necessary, to all new fathers a post-natal 'Fathers Pack' which gives information on Sure Start and its activities in a father-friendly way.

Key issues for reflection

- Do you actively include fathers in antenatal working and if so, how?
- How many of the strategies described above do you use in your service?
- Which of the above strategies could you easily introduce into your provision and how?

Challenges and ways forward

Services intending to develop cohesive antenatal and post-natal 'father work' need to address a number of challenges. To do so will require the participation of all service members and will take a significant investment of time, energy and leadership to do so. The development of the work needs to address issues faced by the service itself, the mothers who use the service and the fathers themselves.

There are seven key challenges:

- *Gaining acceptance among the agencies' female staff and other workers that male involvement is desirable and safe.*

If a number of the workforce have personal experiences of men that has involved domestic/family violence, this may impact on their ability to work with or welcome men into their working environment. The issues of personal safety, comfort and experience will need to be sensitively discussed and explored among the whole team.

Senior managers and team leaders have the ability to engender work with men but it should also be recognized that they have the ability to block work also. The senior workers in organizations have similar experiences of men as those of the teams they manage and they must also be actively involved in the above processes.

- *Gaining acceptance among the female users of the agencies' premises, activities and resources that male involvement is desirable and safe.*

It should be noted that a substantial number of the prime users of the services will probably be women and they too will have the same issues as the workers. They may view the organization as a 'safe haven' from men or as an opportunity to discuss issues relating to men. Opportunities to discuss and resolve these issues, in a supportive and structured way, should be offered.

- *Gaining acceptance among partner agencies that the work you intend to do reflects strategic thinking and working.*

If other agencies are working towards differing goals or objectives regarding working with fathers and men, there is a potential for conflictual working. It would be advisable to 'map' present services offered to, and activity surrounding fathers in your locality and engage with those groups whose agendas or strategic thinking may differ from yours.

- *Combating the negative images of men in the media and engendering a whole agency approach to normalizing male participation in services*

As we saw in Chapter 1, the media portrayal of men has not, on the whole, been positive or supportive. Men are aware of such portrayals and need reassurance that the agency and its users value and respect them in their role as father or carer of their children. To do this requires a planned and careful whole-systems campaign. I would suggest that a 'fathers champion' within a team is an essential first step in developing whole-team working with dads and men.

- *Convincing men that the agencies' premises, activities and resources should be viewed as welcoming space.*

This is a major task and again will require whole-team working. Making premises 'men friendly' and welcoming is not just about putting up a few posters and setting up a sports event. It involves policy shift and change that remove barriers to male participation. Clear statements that men are valued and they matter should be displayed and included in all literature and materials produced.

- *Raising awareness among the fathers in the community that the agency has something to offer them.*

This needs to be done in a timely and sensitive way. A careful advertising/publicity campaign which informs men of the benefits and opportunities you offer needs to be developed. All members of the agency, including reception staff and ancillary staff, need to be able to clearly articulate to fathers and mothers what will be gained by fathers if they take up the services offered.

- *Involving male users in activities that contribute to the meeting of agencies' targets and objectives.*

Men impact on issues such as post-natal depression, infant feeding and all other aspects of child care and are, on the whole, the main supporter of their partner. It is important that agencies view fathers as a valuable resource in the antenatal period. It may be of value to develop methods of working that enable your agency to deliver services and activities which are timely and relevant to the situation your target group are in. For example, the antenatal period is a good time to offer a meaningful service to new dads as this can lead to normalization of their attendance at agencies' activities and lead to increased attendance when other services are offered.

Key issue for reflection

- What can your service do to ensure that fathers can undertake the *'singular most important form of human interaction'* to the best of their abilities?

Conclusion

The issues outlined above are not a comprehensive list of those that will or may impact on your agency. They are suggested starting points from which to begin working. The issues raised may, for some, be seen as contentious and too sensitive to address. Deciding if, or how, your agency will attend to these and other issues will require careful consideration and the involvement of a senior manager to ensure the process goes smoothly and sensitively.

Finally, it should be remembered that including fathers in antenatal and post-natal services is not optional. The Gender Equality Bill (2007) states:

> Men are disadvantaged by workplace cultures that do not support their families or childcare responsibilities, by family services that assume they have little or no role in parenting, or by health services which do not recognize their different needs.
>
> The Gender Equality Bill makes it a legal requirement for service providers to design 'services with the different needs of men and women in mind' (chapter 1, para. 10).

5

Engaging Fathers in Early Years Settings

Tim Kahn

Chapter Outline

Introduction

Over the last decade or so, as a result of changing social and economic circumstances, new legislation and changing attitudes, practitioners in early years settings have attempted to engage with fathers as well as mothers, though often with limited success. This chapter will explore the following issues:

- Why it is important to involve fathers in early years settings
- How involved fathers currently are in early years settings
- What the barriers to fathers' involvement in these settings are
- How we can engage fathers effectively in early years play settings.

Why involve fathers in early years settings?

There are a whole host of benefits arising out of father involvement with their young children. As we saw in Chapter 1, researchers have found that children whose fathers are involved with them when they are young do better at school and have better mental health even after other factors such as fathers' socio-economic status and education have been taken into account (Flouri and Buchanan, 2004). Although this book is not the place to discuss all of the intricacies of the potential benefits (and costs) of father involvement (see Burgess, 2008 for a full discussion), the following statement in the *National Service Framework for Children, Young People and Maternity Services* in 2004 sums up the benefits of father involvement as follows:

> … positive involvement by fathers in their children's learning is associated with … better mental health, higher quality of later relationships, less criminality, better school attendance and behaviour, and better examination result (DH, 2004, standard 2, paragraph 2.2)

Research by Desforges and Abouchaar (2003, p. 24) indicated that what parents do with their children at home '*is most closely associated with [children's] better attainment in the early years*'. Then the EPPE (Effective Preschool Provision in Education) research indicated that the early home learning environment was the key factor in determining the outcomes for children in their current and future lives. Although EPPE did not break down the home learning environment into the impact of mothers and fathers and other family members, this is still an important piece of research in relation to our story here.

Recognizing that early years settings need to support the home learning environment, they need to engage with fathers as well as mothers, both in cases where parents are living together and where parents are living apart from one another and children are in contact with both parents. In the latter case, it needs to be recognized that the home learning environment may be based in two or more places, so efforts need to be made to engage with the separated parent. Practice has shown this to be more challenging, though, we would argue, still essential (see Chapter 10 for more on engaging separated fathers).

How involved are fathers in early years settings?

It is difficult to say how involved fathers are in early years settings at this present time. Research by Page et al. (2008) described involvement of fathers in services as 'sporadic'. In some places the authors identified excellent practice, usually '*the result of specific managers and practitioners taking an interest in the issue.*' In 2006, a National Audit Office review of children's centres found that they were much more effective at engaging mothers than fathers.

This discussion also raises the issue of the meaning of 'involvement'. In 2009 the Pre-school Learning Alliance ran a *Dad Challenge* which required early years settings to audit the sex of the person who dropped off or collected their child at the setting. Although only a small number of settings from a range of urban and rural environments participated in the *Dad Challenge* (22), 18 settings sent in their completed audit forms. These showed that the number of males who collected or dropped off children ranged between 10 to 40%, averaging at almost 25% (Kahn, 2009). Similar figures have been obtained from other settings which have undertaken such an audit, suggesting that a sizeable minority of people dropping off children at settings are fathers (and other male caregivers). We would suggest that such men are 'ripe' for involvement although (anecdotally) practitioners might not 'see' them until they are 'involved' in a formal programme. We think, in line with research carried out by the University of Derby and the Pre-school Learning Alliance, that it would be useful for practitioners to broaden their focus from just engaging with fathers in a formal way, to using every moment to engage with fathers when they are present at settings (Sanders et al., 2008).

Barriers to fathers' involvement

There are a range of barriers which serve to deter fathers and male carers from becoming involved in early years settings and the most common of these are explored below.

What's in a name?

In the second half of the 1980s, when my children were young, I sometimes took them to what was then called a 'mother and toddler group'. I did not feel that the name of the group was inviting to me – a father – but then neither did the name welcome the person (female) who normally took them – a childminder. A growing number of these parent and toddler groups are now called 'Stay and Play' or 'Baby and Toddler' groups – as there is no one word that can describe the adult who stays with the child who may be a parent, a grandparent, a childminder or some other person who is close to the child, and may of course be male or female. In other words, when thinking of a name for your group, think inclusively and – in our case – think about how a father or male caregiver would respond to the name.

A female environment

Although the names of some groups, and the titles of many who work in the early years, have become more gender neutral (early years practitioner rather than Nursery Nurse, for example), the gender make-up of people who get involved in a hands-on way with services is changing much more slowly. Claire Cameron and colleagues from the Institute of Education University of London (2002), argued that early years childcare is still perceived as 'substitute mothering'. This is despite the social and economic changes that have taken place which have led more mothers with young children into the workforce and shifted responsibility for the early years clearly into education. But childcare is still primarily associated with something that mothers do.

'Just talk normally to us!'

In some settings, fathers who drop off and collect their children from their setting report that some staff do not talk to them in the same way as they talk to (most) mothers. The following is part of the transcript of a focus group discussion interview with a group of fathers as part of some research that the Pre-school Learning Alliance carried out in 2005:

> *Father:* When my wife was working, some days I used to take A- to her nursery – we only managed to make that work if one of us took her and the other one picked her up. I found it amazing that even though there were quite a lot of dads doing either the drop off or the pick up, nursery staff just did not talk to us at all in the same way as they would talk to mums. It was very, very difficult to get even basic information out from them about how the day had gone, even though I felt I was a regular person doing that (Kahn, 2009).

> **Key issues for reflection**
> - Is there any difference in the ways in which your staff talk to mothers and fathers?
> - What are the differences?
> - How might you address any differences which exist?

The culture of groups

All groups have a particular culture or way of behaving and doing things which may include or exclude those attempting to join them. For example, within most groups there are generally unwritten and accepted rules about a number of things, such as how people talk to each other and what they talk about, how they make decisions or respond to newcomers. Where the composition of groups is largely single sex, then particular issues may arise for members of the opposite sex attempting to join in. Stories vary about the involvement of fathers and grandfathers in baby and toddler groups. In some cases, these male carers are well integrated into the fabric of groups, whereas in other groups male and female carers hardly mix. There may be many reasons for this, and it is helpful to look at how both the males and the females behave in the group to understand what in the dynamic of the group needs to change in order for male carers to be better integrated. Do remember, though, that it is the majority – that is, the female carers – who have a key role in creating the culture in 'their' group. It is easy to focus on the 'problem' of the minority group, when the cause of the 'problem' may lie to a great extent with the majority.

> **Key issues for reflection**
> - What kind of culture is there in the groups your service runs?
> - How might the culture of groups deter men from taking part?
> - How could you address any barriers which might exist?

Approaches to effective engagement with fathers

The following represent a range of possible approaches to engaging fathers or male carers in early years settings.

Where to start: a review of the current situation

Remember that the setting needs to prepare its environment to ensure that it is father-friendly. So there is preparatory work that must be done before fathers can be expected to come through the door. A good place to start is with reflection.

Reflective practice encourages practitioners to look critically at their work and themselves and to honestly evaluate their strengths and areas for development. Ask yourself, and that includes your whole staff team, how effectively your service engages with fathers, and how you feel about fathers. You will need to think about the following issues.

What kind of father?

It is useful to look at the statistics that are produced by your local authority to gain information about fathers and families locally, so that you can base your work with fathers on actual data rather than on assumption. The data may, for example, tell you that you live in an area where there is high male unemployment and thus you may choose to focus particularly on engaging with unemployed fathers. You may choose to target fathers from minority ethnic communities, non-resident fathers or young fathers. Looking at local data will help you decide which fathers you want to focus on. This is important as it will affect which organizations you choose to partner with and which fathers you consult with to ask what would interest them and what activities you actually provide.

Consulting with fathers

It is dangerous to assume that all fathers are interested in the same thing – for example, football or computers. In reality, some fathers like football whereas others do not. Just like mothers, fathers are individuals and need to be treated as such. So, rather than putting on the activity that *you* think will interest local fathers, and then when you conclude after none (or few) attend that fathers are just not interested, it makes more sense to ask them first what *they* want and to try to provide activities that match their interests. They may want ball-skills sessions with their young children but equally they may say that they would like a family outing for the whole family. Listen openly to what they say and interpret it in the light of your knowledge and understanding of local families and local circumstances. In the same way that you may think of yourself as a resource to mothers and children, involving fathers means thinking of yourself as a resource to the whole family – and this means having fathers in mind whether you meet them or not, and whether they share the same home as their child who uses your setting, or not.

Key issue for reflection

- How will you go about finding out what might encourage fathers in your area to get involved in your setting?

Audit

As was highlighted in Chapter 3, collecting information on fathers is an important starting point. You might like to audit the gender of those who may be involved in your setting in various ways to gain some initial idea about the number of male carers who have any contact with your service. If there is a substantial number of male carers, you may choose to develop a strategy to engage with those who already come to the setting. The audit may 'tell' you something different if there are few male carers attending. Use the information that you glean from the audit to help you decide on a strategy for engaging with fathers.

At the Pre-school Learning Alliance, we have designed a simple audit form for busy practitioners to use; it has been designed with manageability in mind and can be adapted, if necessary, to fit your circumstances. So, while it has been designed initially for childcare settings where children are left by their parents and carers, it can be adapted for use in baby and toddler groups (where parents and carers stay with their young children), or other early years services. You can find a link to a Word copy of the Audit – entitled Dad Challenge Audit Form – on the fathers page of the Pre-school Learning Alliance website (http://www.pre-school.org.uk/practitioners/inclusion/380/engaging-fathers). The audit suggests that staff keep a tally of the following:

- How many mothers/fathers drop off their children at the start of sessions?
- How many mothers/fathers stay for any part or whole of a session during the week?
- How many mothers/fathers collect their children at the end of sessions?

The value in carrying out an audit is that it can give you a picture of actual reality which may differ from what you think may be reality and in fact is a false assumption.

Key issue for reflection

- Do you know how many fathers/male carers are involved in any aspect of your setting?
- Could you carry out a simple audit, such as that suggested above within the next month?
- What could you do with such information?

A father-inclusive environment

Images on the wall of men (as well as women) with children are essential – it is really helpful for all users (and, in this case, fathers) to see themselves reflected in the environment. An absence of male images speaks loudly.

Do consider items such as reading material aimed at fathers (as well as at mothers) in the parents' area, a notice-board for fathers, a gender-neutral appearance to the setting which does not discourage fathers from attending and this includes the colour of the paint on the walls. You could ask yourself and ask fathers (and mothers) who bring their children to the setting, in what ways the environment of the setting could be improved to be more attractive and welcoming to fathers?

Father-inclusive language

The P-word is the 'parent' word. Evidence from a number of practitioners suggests that the word 'parent' in the context of early years and family services is often heard by both mothers and fathers as 'mother'. An example of this is the letter to parents that a child may bring home from their setting. The mother sees the letter first and may not show the letter to the father (both if they are living together or apart) unless she thinks it will be of particular interest to him. This is not malicious censorship but pragmatic sorting. It reflects the fact that historically it has been predominantly mothers who have generally looked after young children and that trying to include fathers in services is rather like swimming against a cultural tide which assumes that mothers are the natural carers of children. If, on the other hand, the letter is headed 'Dear mothers and fathers', it is more likely that the letter will reach him.

It is good practice to think about all your communication with parents. There is such a plethora of family members who are involved in the care of children, that it would be churlish to have a long and complete list that included grandparents, aunts and uncles, older sibling and so on. The point we are making is that it is important to acknowledge male carers in the communication because otherwise there is a good chance that they will be overlooked.

Thus, we would recommend that you include the F-word (the father word) in your verbal and written communication with parents and that you remember to use the F-word in your posters, on your notice-boards and in your electronic communication, including websites.

Having thought about the parent and father words, we would suggest you think more generally about language. Certain words and phrases seem to be effective with women but not with men, and vice versa. Thus, for example, the term 'support group' is likely to have a greater appeal to many women who are more open to sharing ideas and learning informally from one another, whereas the term 'advice session' is more likely to appeal to many men with their often greater interest in solutions to concrete problems. The activities publicized as 'support groups' or 'advice sessions' can be identical, but using different words to publicize them can appeal particularly to women or men. An invitation to 'come in for a cuppa and a chat' may appeal to many women but its open-endedness can act as a deterrent for men, whereas being asked to help out with a particular job may feel more welcoming (and more achievable) to many men.

Historically, the clients of the early years (and family) services have mostly been mothers and other female carers and children. Concepts and language have unintentionally developed in a way that appeals to women. Thus we need to reflect on the language and concepts that we use and try to ensure that we balance our appeal to women and men.

Other examples of female and male language are:

Female	Male
Child development course	Course on the nuts and bolts of kids
Parenting course	Stress management for families
Talking about issues	Solving problems

> **Key issues for reflection**
>
> Think about the language that you use to involve parents in your setting:
> - How do fathers respond to it?
> - How could you make your verbal and written language more father-inclusive?

You will think of other words and concepts that work in your locality. Because of the historical development of different areas, there are likely to be regional variations in what works for women and men.

Timing and venue

Think about the timing of and venue for events. If many of the local fathers are in employment, then it is unlikely that they could attend activities that take place on a weekday. However, activities that take place at the weekend may be more accessible for them. Bear in mind the possibility that fathers who are out of work may not want to publicize this fact by attending events that take place during the week, though others working shifts may welcome the opportunity.

Early years settings have traditionally been seen as 'female spaces' and although this is changing as more fathers and other male carers take their children to pre-school or nursery or stay with their children in baby and toddler groups, they are still predominantly female spaces. Some men, perhaps those who lack the most confidence and are least outgoing, may be reluctant to cross the invisible barrier into the early years setting. Thus it is important to think about the venue where an activity takes place and to consider whether it could take place in a more gender-neutral or male-inclusive environment.

Thus, for example, if you particularly wanted to attract fathers to a meeting for parents, you could hold it in a pub, a place where often men commonly feel comfortable. Another idea that Milton Keynes Pre-school Learning Alliance use, is that they run a monthly Pushchairs in the Park activity that routinely attracts some 50 adults (with their young children) of whom about one-third are male.

Case Study: using a neutral venue

Pushchairs in the Park started over ten years ago. Every month, under-fives are invited to bring their carers for a walk and take part in activities along the way. Each monthly event takes place in a different park around Milton Keynes and attracts local residents, many of whom will come to every event across the city. For the last few years, over 100 people have been attracted to each event, with an equal split of adults and children.

The event is fully outdoors which means there is no limit to the number of people who can be accommodated. Everybody loves coming out on a sunny day, but the children especially love it when it rains ... for the puddles!

An unintended, and added, bonus is a good proportion of fathers come, often representing a third of the adults. This is normally unheard of at an early years event, apart from at sports days and nativity plays. It was not planned that way, it just happened. The men say that they like these events because they are in open spaces and are welcoming, and they don't feel under pressure to make conversation or take part in craft-related activities.

Making men feel like they belong in your setting

You could ask yourself how comfortable you (and your staff) feel about conversing with fathers. I remember that when I taught five-year-olds in a school, I learned about the current craze (which, at that time, was Pokemon) so that I could converse with the children on 'their' territory. Do you need to do your own 'homework' on certain topics so that you can converse comfortably with all fathers on 'their' territory? Recognize that fathers may feel uncomfortable until you have made them feel welcome in the early years environment. Their banter or their testing out of you may be their way of checking out how comfortable you feel with them. Once they feel at ease with you, they may relax and show you a different, even a more vulnerable side of themselves. Remember that it is difficult for many men to show vulnerability because, however much an individual man accepts or rejects cultural images of how a man is supposed to behave, the dominant image of the man who can do things and does not show his vulnerability does generally influence all men.

Case Study

This is a description of how the staff in one setting relate to the parents of the children who use the setting, and in particular to fathers.

'We learned that one of the children's fathers is a Tottenham Hotspur football supporter and so we joke with him about his team's performance on the previous weekend. This exchange fits into our setting's whole-team strategy for getting to know fathers and mothers. We make an extra effort to include male carers as it is something we feel strongly about. We do this by having a list of all of the children's mothers', fathers' and main carers' names up in our storage cupboard so when a child's parent comes to collect them we can use their name instead of "Sam's Mum" or "Sam's Dad". This does help especially if a dad comes to collect their child who is not normally the main collector.'

Men's 'comfort zones' is a concept that is talked about by those who work in this field. What we mean in this context is activities that are more likely than not to appeal to many men and are set up with men in mind. So, this is not trying to be stereotypical in its approach, but being realistic in recognizing that many men might initially be more interested in rocket-making or martial arts (to pick two examples) and, through offering men-father-friendly activities, there is more chance of initially getting fathers involved. This approach is based on the idea that if a particular group is not using or is under-using services, rather than calling that group 'hard to reach' and carrying on offering the same services in the same ways as previously, it makes more sense to adapt services (making them 'easier to reach') to the needs and interests of the target group (in this instance fathers) that they are trying to engage.

Comfort zone examples to attract fathers:

- organizing a regular breakfast for fathers and their children on a weekday, or a regular group for fathers and their children on a weekend
- running family learning sessions on a topic that may particularly interest fathers such as science or woodworking – the session could be for fathers only or could be advertised as 'fathers particularly welcome'
- organizing sessions on topics such as martial arts and/or computer skills, that may appeal to men/fathers, rather like yoga and baby massage that have tended to appeal to women/mothers
- asking fathers to help with DIY or developing the garden, using any skills that they might have. *Remember, that father involvement may begin, but by no means should end, here.* After a father has been in to help the setting with his skills, encourage him to get involved in activities with the children.

Remember that your ultimate goal is the inclusion of all groups of people into the mainstream of your service. In this instance, this will mean encouraging fathers to move beyond their comfort zone when they are ready into mixed-sex groups. We would argue that fathers and other caregivers will happily embrace the mainstream activities that your setting puts on once they see that the service is for them as well as for female carers. However, it may be necessary to prepare more female dominated groups for the arrival of fathers, by giving group members an opportunity to discuss this development beforehand.

Key issues for reflection

- What kinds of activities could you begin to develop for fathers/male carers in your setting?
- What additional resources might you require to develop such activities?

First contacts: introductory events

Ensure that invitations to introductory events for parents whose children are starting at an early years setting are addressed to mothers and fathers (not just 'parents'). In the case, where parents are living apart, ensure that the non-resident parent (usually the father) knows about the introductory session and is given the opportunity to attend. Special arrangements for non-resident parents may need to be made as there may still be tensions between parents who are separated – thus it may be easier for them to attend separate introductory events.

More fathers seem to be attending introductory events (usually with their child's mother) than previously, but their continued engagement at the setting is infrequent, as previously. Thus, we would suggest putting energy into maintaining the setting's ongoing relationship with both mothers and fathers.

Case study: a setting that ensures that working with fathers is a central part of its partnership work with parents.

Afternoon introductory sessions for parents of children who are going to start in our pre-school are an opportunity for parents to come and visit the pre-school, to find out all about us and for their children to play. It seemed natural to invite both mothers and fathers, and letters were always personally addressed to the respective parents. Being aware of the

> diverse family make-up in today's society, we now ensure that when the initial appointment is made, we ask who the letter should be addressed to and take the father's availability into account to emphasize that we like to include fathers from the beginning. We find that about a third of fathers attend this initial meeting.
>
> Meeting and involving fathers right from the start has a huge impact on our relationship with them and on the children in our care and this has helped to ensure that our strong whole-family ethos continues.

Exploring staff attitudes

Any difficulties in engaging men in your service *may* in part be the result of underlying feelings about men that affect you and/or your staff team. If, for example, you are offering a range of 'father-inclusive' activities, but these are poorly attended, then you may need to ask yourself whether, despite apparently positive intentions, you are in fact communicating a mixed message about welcoming fathers. Thus you could ask yourself questions such as: 'How welcoming am I able to be towards the fathers who drop off their children?' 'Do I feel more comfortable with some fathers than others, older rather than younger fathers, for example?

Key issues for reflection

- What do you know about the attitudes of your staff towards fathers/male carers?
- How might you find out what these are in a non-judgemental way?

Confronting issues of sexuality and other uncomfortable issues

Sexuality is another area that can go unacknowledged in early years services. Once services with a predominantly female staff start to engage with men, in this case fathers, sexual frissons are more likely to occur. It is helpful to recognize in advance that this may happen and be prepared for it if it does. Rather than dismissing flirty behaviour between female staff and male parents by saying that it is unprofessional and that 'it doesn't happen here', acknowledge and explore such issues with your staff.

It may also be useful for you (and your colleagues) to explore your feelings and relationships with your own fathers, and your male partners or ex-partners, if you have one, as this may, consciously or unconsciously, affect the way you relate to other fathers. There may be simple correlations such as a difficult relationship with your own father that may make it hard for you to relate well to other fathers.

The aim of your reflections is to ensure that the service as a whole, and you in particular, are welcoming towards all users, including fathers/male carers. Historically fathers may sometimes have been seen as a 'risk' by family services. In fact, fathers need to be seen as a 'resource', while of course recognizing that a small minority of fathers, through their violent and abusive behaviour do pose a risk, as is discussed elsewhere in this book.

Key issues for reflection

- How welcoming of fathers is your service?
- What could you change in order for your service to be more welcoming of fathers?

Non-resident fathers

Remember that some of the children who use your early years service may be living in separated families. It is important that you think about non-resident as well as resident fathers. For more on approaches to working with non-resident fathers see Chapter 10.

Working with mothers

You could be forgiven for thinking that father work is solely focused on working with men. However, mothers play a central part in this area of work, either as enablers or as impeders. The concept of mothers as gatekeepers of caring is a widely accepted phenomenon (see Goldman, 2005). Some mothers may not want their male partners to 'interfere', when it comes to caring for children, while others consciously want their male partners to do more. A third category may feel that they want their male partners to take a more active part in caring for their children but may be reluctant to discuss the issue of childcare with them, for a variety of reasons.

The situation is, of course, very complex. However, it is important to encourage mothers to be 'gate-openers' rather than 'gate-closers'. This may require settings to encourage informal or, if necessary, formal discussions with mothers to support initiatives to engage with fathers/male carers.

> **Key issue for reflection**
>
> How can your setting encourage mothers to play an active role in encouraging fathers to get involved in your setting?

Taking a proactive stance

To conclude this section on approaches to working with fathers/male carers, a key point to emphasize is that to engage effectively with fathers, as with any group that under-uses services, a proactive and persistent strategic stance is needed. As long as you take no action and merely hope that more fathers start using your service, this is unlikely to happen. Some settings report that one year they have a number of fathers involved but then, when this cohort of children and their parents leave the setting, the next year no fathers are involved. In this instance, the involvement of fathers is not strategic; one could describe it as haphazard. What is needed is a strategy to ensure the involvement of fathers is regular and happens year after year.

> **Key issue for reflection**
>
> - Which fathers do and which fathers do not use your setting?
> - What action can you take to enable those fathers who feel like they do not belong in your setting to start participating in your setting's activities?

Conclusion

This chapter has discussed the reasons why it is important for early years services to engage with fathers. It has discussed the barriers that make it difficult for services to engage with fathers and suggested strategies for overcoming them. In essence, it has been argued that early years services have traditionally been used predominantly by mothers and other female carers and are still predominantly female-staffed. Staff in these settings and practitioners in advisory and policy roles need to proactively decide to change the unconsciously female nature of their services so that services become more attractive to male caregivers.

6

Engaging Fathers in Early Years Transitions

Carol Potter, Gary Walker and Bev Keen

Chapter Outline

Introduction

This chapter will draw on our evaluation of a project developed by an expert agency in fathers work, whose aim was to engage fathers and male carers in an area of disadvantage during their children's transition from nursery to reception class. We will discuss what had generally prevented men from getting involved before the project and which strategies were successful in engaging them during it.

Why involve fathers in early years transitions?

As has been evidenced throughout this book, there is no doubt that the positive involvement of fathers in their children's lives is strongly associated with better outcomes for children in a number of key areas, including educational achievement. In relation to this chapter, it is important to note that father involvement in the early stages of their children's learning and education has been found to predict educational attainment at 20 (Flouri and Buchanan, 2004), so it is important for services to support that involvement early on.

We know that fathers from a lower social class are less likely to be involved in their children's education at any point during their children's lives (Flouri and Buchanan, 2003) which compounds the problem of low educational achievement in children from disadvantaged backgrounds (Blanden, 2006). The greater involvement of fathers in the early years could help to improve this situation.

Moving on from the general picture with regard to father engagement within services to the specific area of early educational transition which is the context for the current chapter, it is important to set the scene in relation to this important phase in young children's lives and current approaches to involving fathers within it.

Young children today experience a number of transitions which may include the separation of their parents, moving to new environments and moving between educational settings. These changes can be beneficial for children depending on the level of support which they receive through each. Within an educational context, the transition from early years settings to primary schools settings has been identified as particularly important. Fabian and Dunlop (2006, p. 2) stated:

> The start of primary schooling has been perceived as one of the most important transitions in a child's life and a major challenge of early childhood. Initial success at school both socially and intellectually, leads to a virtuous cycle of achievement.

A number of approaches have been found to be effective in helping young children to negotiate this critical transition successfully, including the use of transitional activities and the active involvement of all of those involved including children, parents, early years and school staff (Sanders et al., 2005).

It is interesting to note that despite the increased emphasis on the importance of fathers in children's lives, there is very little explicit reference to
fathers in research and/or reports on parental involvement in early years
transitions. For example, the government-sponsored report *A Study of the
Transition from Foundation Stage to Key Stage 1*, (Sanders et al., 2005) makes
382 references to 'parents' and only 5 to fathers.

This omission is unfortunate given that we know that by far the most
effective way to recruit and retain fathers is through the use of approaches
specifically tailored to the needs of men (Goldman, 2005). The Fathers
Transition Project, discussed in this chapter, is therefore both innovative
and of particular significance, given the relative dearth of such work in the
research literature and at UK policy level.

Father involvement in schools

With regard to fathers and primary school engagement, it is widely acknowledged that fathers are generally less involved with their children's schools and
learning than mothers (see Goldman, 2005 for an in-depth review). Page and
colleagues (2008) found in their review of 46 local authorities that primary
schools were much more involved with mothers than fathers, although senior
staff especially were aware of the importance of father involvement in relation
to child outcomes. Schools tended to be 'gender neutral' in their approach,
not seeking to use different strategies for engaging men. A recent evaluation
of the Parent Support Adviser role (Cullen et al., 2011) found that PSA's were
much more successful in engaging women rather than men. Major barriers to
father engagement reported by primary school staff included: mostly female
staffing; 'policy overload' making it difficult to have a specific focus on fathers
and difficulties of providing activities for working fathers out of school hours
(Page et al., 2008).

The Fathers Transition Project

The Fathers Transition Project took place in an area of disadvantage in
the North of England. It was developed by an expert agency, with over
ten years experience of working successfully with fathers in a variety of
service settings. The project consisted of three partners working together: a
part-time dedicated male fathers worker from the agency, a children's centre
and primary school, based on the same site. Fathers were recruited before
the summer holidays, with the intention that they would become engaged

with the school when their children transferred to mainstream school. As researchers, we talked to staff and fathers involved with the project to gain their views on barriers to father engagement and how these were overcome within the Fathers Transition Project.

Barriers to father involvement before the Transitions Project

Children's centre

Before the Fathers Transition Project began, children's-centre staff identified a range of possible barriers to fathers using children's centre services. Most staff felt that one of the key reasons for low male attendance at activities was related to their work. Men who are in employment could not come to sessions during the normal working week but in addition, many men in the area worked shifts and this was thought to have affected their ability and willingness to attend activities which they could not participate in on a regular basis.

Other reasons given by staff for lack of father involvement have been referred to in other chapters, such as that some men might feel uncomfortable in sessions mostly attended by women. In addition, given the traditional nature of the area, some men might continue to see going to child-related activities as 'women's work'.

School setting

The Fathers Transition Worker discussed several possible reasons why fathers in the area might not want to become closely involved with their children's school. They may have had difficulties themselves at school and/or may experience literacy problems which might significantly affect their willingness to enter that environment. Their confidence and self-esteem might therefore be low.

Project outcomes

How much father involvement was there during the project?

The Fathers Transition Project was successful in working with a group of fathers during the period of their children's transition from the nursery to the reception class. It is important to note that these were men who had not been involved with any kind of family-related service before. A total of 76 father or male-carer attendances were recorded on Transition Project trips and activities. Of these 60 were recorded on trips and 16 on centre and school-based activities. There were approximately 95 mother attendances on the same activities.

The total number of father/male-carer attendances at the three *school-based* events was 19.

Key issues for reflection

- Does your service keep a detailed record of father attendances at a range of activities?
- Can you distinguish between the number of fathers who have attended a range of activities, as opposed to the number of father attendances there have been overall?

Benefits of the Fathers Transition Project

Fathers and staff identified a wide range of benefits from their involvement with the Fathers Transition Project. Specifically they talked about the following;

- enjoyment for children and fathers
- opportunities for new experiences for men and children
- support for relationships between fathers and children
- better opportunities for men to be involved in their children's play and learning
- increased confidence for men.

What some fathers said about their engagement in their children's play and learning was especially important:

> ... now on a night ... It is enjoying these times with the bairn ... when I was a young one I found it difficult to read out loud, but because of these groups, I am wanting to get more involved – these groups are making me want to – I am reading to her and she loves it – I read her a bedtime story

> [We were] building a little den in the woods – finding twigs and building it up and then looking at the tracks of the animals and it was just hours together – just me and him. It was fantastic – a beautiful day – he loved it.

One of the school staff involved in the project said:

> [When fathers were involved] children actually were more engaged for longer

on activities … the level of conversation between parents and children was improved. I think in the past, and even today, when mums and dads come together, dads naturally stand back and let the mothers do the conversation … So the conversation has improved, having the dads in to actually do an activity with the children.

It is clear from the comments above that fathers and children benefited significantly and in a number of ways from the activities provided by the Fathers Transition Project. These are the kinds of benefits which are likely to contribute to better outcomes for children in future. For more discussion on the benefits of the Fathers Transition Project, see the whole report (Potter et al., 2009) online at www.fathersplus.org/transitions.

What worked in engaging fathers?

Given the success of the project, we go on next to describe those approaches and strategies which were effective in getting fathers involved.

Strategic level

At a strategic level, the Transition Project was funded by the local County Council who paid for the half-time fathers worker. The need for senior management to support fathers work with adequate resources has been discussed elsewhere in the book.

Partnership working with an expert agency

The Transition Project was devised and implemented by an expert agency in the field of fathers work. The project was therefore able to draw on a range of in-depth knowledge and expertise developed over a long period.

Key issue for reflection

- Could your service find ways of working with expert agencies/advisors in the field of fathers work?

A gender-differentiated approach

Under the guidance of the expert agency, the project adopted a gender-differentiated approach which is widely known to be effective in engaging men. As has been referred to previously, a gender-differentiated approach recognizes that men and women are likely to have different needs and interests and these will need to be addressed differently. As discussed in Chapter 2, this approach was enshrined within the legal framework with the introduction of the Gender Equality Duty (2007) which requires services to take account of the gender differences in the process of service delivery.

In the project being discussed here, gender differentiation meant that the way in which the Fathers Transition Worker talked to men and the kinds of activities used to recruit and retain men, were specifically male orientated. Tim Kahn talks about working with men and language issues in Chapter 5.

Key issues for reflection

To what extent does your service adopt a gender-differentiated approach:
- In its advertising?
- In staff communication with men?
- In the types of activities offered to men?

Skills and abilities of the Fathers Transition Worker

The single biggest factor identified by fathers and staff as crucial in the development of the project was the professional skill of the dedicated Fathers Transition Worker. A number of qualities were identified as being important in enabling the worker to interact successfully with men, namely:

- expertise in working with men
- approachability
- friendliness
- a respectful approach
- trustworthiness
- persistence
- patience
- the ability to listen and to talk to people as individuals.

Fathers and male carers were extremely positive about the Transition Worker's approach. One father commented on his friendliness and trustworthiness:

> I think it is because [he] is welcoming, he is very friendly. As a bloke he talks at my level anyway. When he is speaking to you, he doesn't speak down to you, he doesn't talk over the top of you, and he always has time to listen to you. He is a

> friendly lad and maybe people confide in him … he is a good socializer – he gets
> people involved – he has time for people and I think that's what it is.

Another father commented on his first experience of meeting the Fathers
Transition Worker, emphasizing the informal nature of his approach:

> When I first took me bairn to school … he just came up – you know he was
> approaching the fathers … just like having a chat … but he wasn't like when he
> came – he wasn't like in your face … you know what I mean.

The worker's ability to communicate with people effectively was highlighted
by another man:

> [He] is a good bloke. I found it easy. [He] explains stuff in English – in plain
> English. No offence against people who have been to college and university but
> some professional people do not know how to explain stuff to ordinary people.

Key issue for reflection

- How comfortable are your staff talking to fathers?
- What could you learn from this Fathers Worker's approach?

Hook and male-orientated activities

The project under discussion here used the notion of 'hook' activities to draw
men into the project during the summer months. Hook activities are those
which are intended to be high interest and specifically designed to try to
appeal to men. Practitioners expert in working successfully with fathers and
male carers will often say that the most difficult part of engaging with men
is the first step of 'getting them through the door'. Therefore, at this crucial
stage, it is vital to use high interest, male-orientated activities to increase the
likelihood that men will be tempted to come along. The hope is that if men
can be drawn in using such activities to begin with, then services can then
develop approaches to try to keeping them involved later on.

In the Fathers Transition Project, 'hook' activities took the form of trips to
such venues as a mining museum, a lighthouse and a farm. Alongside these,
were other male-orientated practical activities, such as shelter building on a
forest trip and making a bird box. Fathers clearly enjoyed these activities as
indicated above. School staff felt that this emphasis on 'hands-on, physical,
outside-type things' were important because it was then possible to present

such activities as needing men to be involved, that men had something specific to offer at such events.

Recruiting men

Once hook activities had been developed, the next step was to contact men in such a way that they will then go on to take part in an activity. For many men, taking part in such activities and events will be a completely new experience and therefore persuading them to take part for the first time, often requires great skill. The Fathers Transition Worker was extremely experienced in this area and explained how he approached this task.

Face-to-face contact: valuing fathers

The Worker stated that face-to-face contacts were by far the most effective. The use of leaflets in settings did not recruit a single father. Initial contacts with men were often made in the school playground as men were dropping children off for nursery. The Fathers Transition Worker emphasized the importance of an informal, conversational approach where he was, importantly, asking fathers for their help. Putting the men in the position of being an authority on their local area resulted in a respectful approach where men felt that their opinion was being valued.

> You have to have the skill of being able to talk to people. You have got to show some interest in them. They have some value ... so I am just making friends and asking for assistance and they appreciate that. So that is what I would do, asking them to help.

One school staff member felt that the approach used in the project:

> Boosted [men's] self-esteem of actually being needed, because a lot of these dads don't work for a variety of reasons, including disability.

As discussed above, in Chapter 1, fathers may often experience a deficit model of fatherhood approach where their contribution to raising children can be undermined by assumptions of lack of willingness or competence. The Fathers Transition Worker emphasized the need to build up men's self-esteem to begin with, especially those who may have had poor experiences of education. Starting from a position which explicitly conveys to men what they have to offer is therefore a key approach. Many men are very unlikely to respond positively to an approach which portrays them in need of help and support.

Making relationships

This focus on respect and making relationships at an individual level with fathers was believed to be extremely important in developing trust between the worker and the fathers. It was seen as the first step in persuading men that they may want to engage in an activity which the Fathers Transition Worker was running.

The Fathers Transition Worker also met fathers in the local community by walking around the housing estates and chatting informally to men as they washed cars or, on the Traveller site, were working on caravans. Before trying to make contacts within the Traveller community, he did some initial research on bow-top caravans so that he would have an initial shared point of interest. Such an approach is clearly time-consuming and expensive. However, this kind of community development-based approach is known to be successful in engaging those who may not have been involved with services before, or for whatever reason may be suspicious of them. One father we spoke to admitted to being reluctant about becoming involved at first:

> I was a bit wary at first ... It's the way like dads are treated – you know what I mean ... like they're an outsider – everything's for mams isn't it – you know there's nowt for fathers.

Key issues for reflection

- To what extent does your service convey to fathers that they are valued and have something to contribute?
- Could you improve on this approach in any way?

Retention: keeping men involved

On-going programme of activities

Once fathers/male carers have begun to attend activities, it is vital then to have a strategy for retaining their involvement, as is discussed in other chapters throughout the book. In relation to the Fathers Transition Project, the worker emphasized that maintaining an on-going programme of activities, *on which fathers themselves had been consulted, was vital,* as Tim Kahn emphasized in Chapter 5. Having the next activity always in view was seen as maintaining the momentum.

Intensive follow-up

To ensure that men stayed in contact, the Fathers Transition Worker followed up those who had been engaged with an intensive series of phone calls and texts. The total number of contacts with men made by the Fathers Transition Worker over the nine-month period was 1,360.

Working with mothers

As other contributors have discussed, the effective engagement of fathers in services will always require successful working with mothers. The Fathers Transition Worker in this project sought to engage fathers and male carers through active engagement with mothers:

> I would say [to the mothers], can you just fill [the form] in I would say these trips are on, and you will be invited as well. So I work through the mams.

One of the children's centre staff who had worked on the summer trips highlighted this aspect of the Fathers Transition Worker's approach:

> He is very approachable. So both dads and their partners. Yes, it was a dads' group but he didn't leave the women out.

Once again, information from engagement records shows the level of ongoing involvement with women, as well as men. This approach can be seen in the large number of contacts made with mothers which totalled 1,260 over the nine-month period of the project.

Focus on development work with fathers

One important issue which the Fathers Transition Worker in this project highlighted, was the need to do more than simply attract men to family-related activities and events. This is without doubt a vital first step but beyond that it is crucial to aim to actively support men in their parenting role. In the Fathers Transition Worker's words:

> My job is to engage [fathers] so we have got to work out if there are activities on a Saturday morning for the kids. We have to work out the next step. It is OK engaging the dads, but we have got to have a purpose for them, otherwise it is just a trip.

The first step in supporting men in this worker's view is to get to know men on an individual basis:

> Every dad is different so every need is different.

From the Fathers Worker's point of view, every father has his own issues which he may or may not need help with. The key thing to note here is that working through these issues is very likely to have a positive impact on men's ability to parent their children more effectively.

> You have got to be skilful and you have got to work with [the men], even if there have been issues. You have to work with them where they are and find out the needs. If you find out the needs, you can find out what's going on.

Getting to know what individual fathers need takes time for in-depth relationship building where trust can develop:

> You are looking for their skills, something that they are confident in, something that they can do – not intellectual – so they are coming in and are at an advantage and not a disadvantage. That is his skill. That is his advantage. You are bringing them in on an advantage, so you are building their self-esteem and you manage that. Ask how do you do that? Can I take a picture of that?

The Fathers Transition Worker also talked about some of the key development issues involved in working with fathers in small groups. There were sometimes important issues to be explored relating to language and how to speak respectfully to each other and to children. He gave an example of a discussion that had occurred during one session:

> I said if someone in the group said, they didn't like your child, your child's manners, then what impact would that have? ... So we had a discussion around how to talk. Those discussions build a strong group. You can build a course out of that easily and that would lead to positive communication and the group being a friendly place, a safe place.

Children's centre staff who attended the summer trips in 2008 observed the difference which this developmental approach had in terms of the quality of interactions between parents and children. One commented:

> It is hard to get [fathers] there but it really seemed to work with these dads. Most of them I didn't know but I have seen a difference with dads that I have worked with before. I have been [on trips before] as a parent myself and these [fathers] seemed to be more willing to spend time with their children than I have seen before. Some of them that have been going before were just going for the trip. This time it was completely different.

Children's centre staff had absorbed the importance of personal engagement with fathers on the summer trips in order to persuade them to become involved later on in the school-based phase of the Transition Project. One member of staff explained:

> [The Fathers Transition Worker's] objectives for all of the [summer] trips was quality time with each of [the fathers] – he wants to get to know them and get to know their background ... you know it's more than just a token 'come on a trip and have a good time over the holidays' he's got to make that relationship with them enough to commit them to go and do what they have to do setting up the parents' group in the school.

This was a crucial aspect of the whole Transition Project; that men engaged before their children's move to the reception class should then continue to be engaged in their children's learning afterwards in the more formal school environment.

Implications for future developments

At the time of writing this book, a wide range of 'austerity measures' were being implemented by a coalition government, many of which will significantly affect service provision to mothers, fathers and children. Given the unlikelihood of sufficient funding to employ specialist Fathers Transition Workers within every primary school, in future, there will need to be a gradual move towards a whole-team approach, for the longer-term sustainability of the work. Within such a model, one member of staff could be delegated to oversee the development of work with fathers with additional support and training, as has occurred in a number of schools (Goldman, 2005). Parent Support Advisers within schools could be key within such a strategy, although early evaluations of the effectiveness of these staff suggest that further training in the engagement of fathers and male carers will be needed.

Conclusion

The Fathers Transition Project discussed above was successful in working with a group of fathers during the period of their children's transition from the nursery to the reception class. Fathers and staff involved in the project identified a range of benefits which they had obtained from their involvement. All fathers spoke of benefits for their children in terms of their enjoyment of related activities. Some also believed that project involvement had helped to improve the quality of their relationships with their children, as well as giving them opportunities to become more closely involved in their children's play. The father engagement achieved during the project was brought about through a highly gender-differentiated approach which recognizes that the needs of men and women are different and need to be addressed differently, the use of male-orientated hook activities and more especially, through the highly skilled approaches of the dedicated Fathers Transition Worker.

Part 3
Diversity in Fatherhood

7

Working with Young Fathers

Nigel Sherriff, Kevin Lowe and Liz McDonnell

This chapter draws on our experience as researchers who have interviewed young fathers and the professionals across the country who work with them.

Chapter Outline

Kevin has managed several research projects relating to young fathers and currently oversees the Young People in Focus Supporting Young Fathers Network microsite www.youngfathers.net/[1]. This site contains a wealth of case studies, including research carried out by Nigel and Liz.

Introduction

In this chapter, we discuss why working with young fathers requires a different approach to working with fathers more broadly. In doing so, we look at barriers and strategies specific to this group of fathers and draw upon academic literature, and case-study material from practitioners.

During the past decade, there has been a steady increase in interest in young parents in the UK and this interest gradually began to include young

---

1 See www.youngfathers.net

fathers. In relation to government policy, for example, the impetus came from the desire to reduce the rates of teenage pregnancy and address social exclusion and potential poor outcomes for children. The increasing interest in young fathers has also been influenced by a substantial and growing evidence base which demonstrates that fathers of all ages have a significant role to play in the development and well-being of their children (e.g. Flouri, 2005; Lamb, 2004). At a practice level, evidence from the Supporting Young Fathers Network and others such as Reeves et al., (2008) shows that local and national initiatives to engage with young fathers directly emerged slowly, but gradually, during this period. The Fatherhood Institute, founded in 1999, also contributed to this process (Fatherhood Institute, 2009).

These positive developments are encouraging, but they must also be kept in perspective. For instance, at a research level, despite the extensive and growing UK literature on fathers generally, there still remains a lack of focus and data on young fathers and/or the partners of teenage mothers. Much less is known about young fatherhood compared with the relatively large body of research that is available on young motherhood, although we are able to present the broad picture that follows.

In 2008, 90,576 births were registered with details of a father aged under 25 years of age (13.6% of total births with a father's details), with 14,050 (2.1%) of these young men being teenagers (Office for National Statistics, 2008). Taking into account the proportion of fathers who are not registered and adding existing young fathers who would still be in this age group, we suggest a 'ballpark' figure for the number of fathers under the age of 25 years in England and Wales as being around 325,000, including approximately 35,000 teenagers of whom over 80% would be aged 18 and 19. Of babies born to teenage mothers, about a quarter of young fathers are aged under 20, around a half are aged 20–25 and a further quarter are aged over 25.

We also know that young fathers share many of the characteristics of young mothers in that they are more likely to come from lower socio-economic groups, from families that have experienced financial difficulties, and are more likely than average to have left school at the minimum school-leaving age (Department for Children, Schools and Families, and Department of Health, 2009). They are also more likely than older fathers (and other young men) to have experienced violent forms of punishment at home, and to have been sexually abused. Additionally, they are more likely than other men to have serious anxiety, depression, and conduct disorders; drink, smoke and misuse other substances and to have higher levels of poor health and nutrition.

The limited information currently available to us about young fathers inevitably masks differences within the overall group such as those between, and within, different ethnic groups, for example. Unfortunately, this can lead to unhelpful speculation about the motives and behaviour of young men that may be based on prejudices. A small study on black young fathers in South London found that the behaviour of the young men confounded the negative stereotypes with the young men committed to involvement in fatherhood and the future care of their children despite the pregnancies having been unplanned (Pollock et al., 2005; see also McDonnell et al., 2009, and Warwick et al., 2011).

In addition to a lack of research and knowledge about young fatherhood, it is also apparent that practice in providing effective support to young fathers lags behind current policy aspirations (Potter and Carpenter, 2008). Work with young fathers in public services generally remains sparse, short-term and patchy in terms of both span and quality (Sherriff, 2007).

Benefits of involving young fathers

The case for involving young fathers in both universal and targeted services is clear on two fronts: the benefits for the child and the benefits for the young parents themselves. In terms of the former, evidence demonstrates that a young father's positive involvement in their child's early life is associated with a range of good outcomes for the babies and children including better cognitive development, improved mental health, higher educational attainment, better relationships with peers, less involvement in crime and substance misuse. Moreover, the converse is also true with low levels of involvement being associated with a range of negative outcomes (Flouri, 2005; Lamb, 2004; Lamb and Lewis, 2004). These findings relate to young fathers in general. Some fathers, like some mothers, do, sadly harm their children, and we explore that issue in the discussion on beliefs about young males and fatherhood later in this chapter.

Although there is a debate about whether the poor outcomes that are associated with teenage mothers and young fathers is related to their age, or whether social disadvantage is the more significant factor, research shows that timely access to appropriate care and support can maximize young people's chances of a positive transition to parenthood (DCSF and DH, 2009).

Indeed, the first national UK Young Fathers Project (YFP), which established young fathers projects in five cities in England, identified the benefits of directing services at young fathers as: increased confidence and self-esteem, better parenting skills and self-control for the fathers, and improved relationships with the children's mothers (Mordaunt, 2005). One of the young fathers made this comment about how the services had helped him in terms of personal development:

> Since I've been coming up here I've got my confidence up. I'm more self-motivated, like I do a lot more stuff now. Before, before I come up here I used to be right down in the dumps, but this project has helped me out a lot. That's the reason why I come up here (Young father).

A Young Fathers Project worker who took part commented in relation to one of the young men:

> Changes that were due to his involvement with the YFP? His relationship with his daughter had really developed, becoming much stronger. He was also much more patient. Although his living arrangements had not changed, his contact with his daughter had become more regular and less likely to be cancelled by his baby's mother (Young fathers worker).

Despite the evidence for involving (young) fathers in services, they continue to remain on the fringes of service provision (Sherriff, 2007). In the next section, we explore some of the reasons for this.

What stops young fathers from using services?

The barriers that tend to get in the way of father involvement more generally are discussed in other chapters in this book. We consider three barriers that appear to have the most impact on young fathers specifically: 1) 'traditional' approaches and practice; 2) beliefs about young fatherhood; and 3) age.

1) 'Traditional' approaches and practice

Evidence suggests that services often exclude young fathers through a combination of 'traditional' mother-focused approaches, ignorance of male perspectives, and sometimes through overt discrimination (Pollock et al., 2005). The focus on mothers is deeply embedded within universal services for children and families and tends to be the 'default position'. Consequently, fathers are excluded in a routine way rather than through conscious action. Indeed, when it is explained to workers that their actions served to exclude fathers they are often shocked to realize what has happened (Quinton et al., 2002). Equally, practitioners who are used to only working with young mothers may not be clear about the relevance of involving young fathers (Burgess, 2006), or be unclear how best to do this (Sherriff, 2007). Even services that routinely have contact with young men such as youth offending teams (YOTs) don't necessarily ask questions about parental status as a matter of course.

As we saw in Chapter 4, antenatal and midwifery services have tended not to routinely identify and engage with fathers and fathers-to-be during the important initial stages of pregnancy and birth, and where this does occur, it tends to result from individual staff taking the initiative, rather than from plans at the heart of the local service.

However, some work with young fathers and young fathers-to-be around overcoming such traditional barriers has started to emerge. For instance, the U-Too project in Wiltshire (White, 2010) runs courses for young mothers-to-be and young fathers-to-be across Swindon and Wiltshire to help them understand their responsibilities and support each other as a family. The director of the project has a specific take on reaching young fathers:

> … as we also run courses for young mums-to-be we have easy access to partners, so they [fathers-to-be] *do not* constitute a hard-to-reach group … (our emphasis)

Key issues for reflection

- How 'traditional' is your organization's approach?
- If you are engaging with young fathers, who is taking the lead? Are particular 'champions' leading the work? What would happen if they left?

2) Beliefs about young males and fatherhood

Negative stereotyping of young fathers has led to 'deficit beliefs' which include notions that young fathers are not interested in their children, are irresponsible, uncaring, and that young mothers may do better if they are not involved, and such beliefs influence professionals. But research evidence strongly contests such views, highlighting barriers such as inadequate housing, low income, and resistance from the mother or mother's family (see Burgess, 2006). Some of our own research has shown that many young men want to become and remain involved in their children's lives, and that fatherhood is viewed as a source of delight and pride:

> The joy has snowballed … I've never felt love that I do for Tiana and Joel and Sophie … you know, and I've never felt a sense of accomplishment … previously compared to things that they do that I have taught them or things that I think they have picked up through my influence … I think it is about the emotions that you feel, really, it opens the floodgates … and everything else, you know, suddenly you are more receptive to things and it is nice (Tom, 25, father of 3; cited from McDonnell et al., 2009, p. 8).

Negative or ambivalent attitudes towards young fathers are influenced by genuine concerns about important issues such as domestic violence, child abuse and violence towards staff; but to what extent are such concerns rooted in evidence?

For domestic violence the gendered picture is fairly clear. Rates of domestic-violence incidents experienced by women are five times greater than for men (Home Office, 2009), with women aged 20–24 reporting the highest rates of assault by an intimate. Also, a quarter of teenage girls (aged 13–17) report some form of intimate-partner violence (Barter et al., 2009). However, some analysts argue that the incidence of domestic violence against young men is significantly underestimated (e.g. Dewar Research, 2011).

For child abuse and violence against staff, the picture is less clear. A review of child deaths and injury through abuse and neglect confirms the vulnerability of children born to young parents, as half of the parents of the children who died were under the age of 25. This is all the more relevant given that only a quarter of children each year are born to mothers in that age group. Yet information about the involvement of fathers in these deaths is unclear, as there is often very little recorded information about the fathers or father figures of the children in such cases (DCSF, 2008) bringing us back to the importance of collecting father information, as discussed in Chapter 3.

So, the picture is mixed in relation to the concerns about violent behaviour by young fathers and data is weak in some important areas. What seems striking though is that despite the reported concern about young fathers, little is often known about them. This emphasizes the need to put energy into *engaging* with young fathers, rather than ignoring them, especially in situations where there is concern about a child's safety (see Warwick et al., 2011).

Key issues for reflection

- What ideas about young men influence how you and others in your organization work?
- Is there dialogue and debate? Is there room for different opinions?

---

3) Age

Men who become fathers at a young age (under 25 years) often face significant additional barriers to accessing services than older fathers, such as difficult and complex relations with the mother and her family, educational and/or employment difficulties, sometimes including behavioural problems. There are further barriers for teenage fathers, whose age is often seen as a marker of irresponsibility. School-age fathers are an almost 'invisible' group, although they periodically receive attention when the press identifies a very young father. Some professionals regard school-age fathers (under age 16) as particularly 'hard-to-reach', or simply 'not out there' (Sherriff, 2007). Certainly, the number of children born to school-age fathers each year is very small (ONS, 2008). We estimate that there are likely to be between 550–650 school-age fathers in England and Wales at any given time. Nevertheless, there will be regional differences in the proportions of school-age fathers that will be relevant for service providers.

Sherriff (2007) identifies the need for provision to be attuned to the different needs of school-age fathers and notes that while there are mechanisms in place to identify and support school-age mothers, this is generally not the case for fathers. However, in Leeds, the Healthy Schools and Wellbeing Service has debunked the 'hard-to-reach' tag by employing a Specialist Learning Mentor to focus on the needs of this group alongside wider work on sex-and-relationships education in schools:

> Many of the young men that I work with will stick with the baby and try their best to get on with the mother – often they need additional support to do that, especially in the early stages (Specialist Learning Mentor).

Key issues for reflection

- How can you make your service more 'young-friendly'?
- What changes might be needed? Think about time, place, approach and other practicalities.

We have seen therefore that three broad issues restrict young fathers' access to services:

1 'Traditional' approaches and practice which focus exclusively on mothers and marginalize the role of fathers.
2 Constructs of young fatherhood which result in *young* males being viewed as having little to offer, and being dangerous.
3 Perceptions about age, which result in school-age fathers being overlooked.

Approaches to working successfully with young fathers

Approaches to supporting young fathers vary considerably depending on aims, values, service type, delivery location, practitioners' skills and structure/form of support. The constraints and targets of specific funding streams also play a part. There has been little formal evaluation of the long-term effectiveness of approaches to support young fathers, although data from professionals on what appears to be promising has gradually emerged and it is covered here under the following headings:

- values and aims
- reaching young fathers
- the structure/form of support.

The material covered in this section is drawn primarily from our own recent research (see McDonnell et al., 2009; Sherriff, 2007 and www.youngfathers.net).

Values and aims

While the agendas of different agencies and individual practitioners vary, certain common values emerge in work with young fathers, including the belief that most young fathers are able to play a positive role in their child's life, and a desire to challenge the negative stereotyping of young men/fathers. These values tend to be informed by the research findings outlined above and are often coupled with personal ideology. Indeed, ideology and 'evidence' are contested, and permeate work in this field. These tensions occasionally surface, especially in relation to concerns about violent behaviour by males. Ideology plays a part in how services develop locally, where champions of work with young fathers, and those resistant or ambivalent, play crucial roles. The gender of staff can influence attitudes, though there is no simple male/

female split. In our work we have come across many women leading the work effectively with young fathers.

The knowledge–values mix translates into aims that generally centre around: improving outcomes for children by empowering disadvantaged young fathers, benefits for the fathers themselves through improved self-confidence and skills which result in improved material circumstances, and improved relations with the child's mother. Experience has shown, as with work with young mothers, that a holistic approach that addresses issues such as: education, training and employment; accommodation; the father's health and well-being; sex and relationships is most effective, rather than a narrow focus on parenting skills.

Some practitioners also have particular values around how best to empower service users that challenge traditional 'expert' approaches. For example, they draw upon models of community development and social action that result in young fathers taking on more formal roles within services to shape and deliver what is on offer. These practitioners see the young people as having expert knowledge, vital skills and potential worth investing in. We discuss this approach more in the section on participatory approaches.

Key issues for reflection

- How do the values/attitudes of staff influence your organization's approach? In what ways? Does the gender mix of staff play a part?
- What support do young fathers actually want or need? Have you consulted with them? If not, how could you go about it?

Reaching young fathers

How to reach young fathers is a key issue when targeted services are first set up, or when universal services make the decision to widen their approach and become father-inclusive. Because the impetus to do this tends to be practitioner-led at first, rather than a response to overt demand, it requires a proactive approach. The overarching message from our work is that networking is essential. Agencies and services need to reach the young fathers through young mothers and mothers-to-be, and also identify where young fathers have possibly been overlooked, yet might be relatively easy to reach.

Agencies targeting young fathers have found that developing strong links with antenatal services is a particularly fruitful way of reaching young fathers-to-be. For example, the New Dad Project run by St Michael's Fellowship in South London works closely with antenatal services at Guy's and St Thomas' hospitals. There is more information about this project in the section below on participatory approaches.

> We reach these young fathers by having a presence at the antenatal clinics – the screenings as well as the education classes … we go where we know expectant young fathers are likely to be (Project Co-ordinator, New Dad Project).

Other routes to young fathers have been through referrals from other professionals such as Connexions personal advisors, health visitors, social workers, teachers, young offending/probation officers, youth workers, plus staff in sports and leisure settings. When services are more established, some young fathers refer themselves, though numbers tend to be low.

Key issues for reflection

- How are you currently reaching young fathers?
- Which organizations/individuals do you need to link up with more?

The structure/form of support

In this section we look at how practitioners work with young fathers. Three different modes have emerged:

1 One-to-one work
2 Group work
3 Participatory approaches.

These approaches are not mutually exclusive, but they do require different skills, and to some extent different values. They represent the current 'state of play' on how support to young fathers is actually delivered.

One-to-one work with young fathers

Often, resource-intensive, one-to-one work is the *only* way some harder-to-reach young fathers will engage with services, at least at first. It can be difficult for young men to 'open up' in group settings. Being able to tailor sessions to individual needs and set personalized targets means that effective work gets done relatively quickly. Work with couples can also be considered as a variant of one-to-one work, and while this is certainly an approach being offered successfully by some services, notably the Family Nurse Partnership (FNP) (Barnes et al., 2009) this appears an underdeveloped aspect of one-to-one work overall.

Skills

Building a positive relationship with young fathers is at the core of one-to-one work. A trusting and open relationship enables young fathers to share their concerns and ask questions that they can't ask anywhere else.

In one-to-one work, practitioners tend to use skills and techniques to build such relationships that are drawn from youth work, advocacy and counselling approaches, and are increasingly informed by 'strengths-based' perspectives. Young fathers need to feel understood and it is important that workers demonstrate that they know or can understand where young fathers are coming from. Often, fathers come to one-to-one work having had very negative experiences of services. It is therefore important to establish rapport with them.

Many of the practitioners actively link positive behaviour in the young fathers with good outcomes for children. Building self-esteem, confidence and skills in young dads can trickle down to their children.

Work with couples requires additional skills. Some practitioners will have this expertise from work as couples' counsellors or as family workers. Others, such as Family Nurses, have training that enables them to work flexibly with couples using tools termed 'facilitators' that are part of the FNP programme, and enable couples to explore a wide range of issues related to bringing up a young child. The long-term benefits of the FNP programme have been well-established via robust research methods in the USA. Implementation in England is still in a relatively early phase and research has focused on how it is being delivered rather than on its impact on young families. Encouragingly, this research has shown that the nurses are engaging with fathers, and the young fathers are generally very positive about what is on offer (Barnes et al., 2009).

Issues covered in one-to-one work

The issues covered in this approach tend to be broad and include: school; work; benefits; housing; pre/post-natal issues; childbirth; child development; basic skills e.g. literacy; and gaining access/contact with children if this is a problem. It is important to note that one-to-one work with young fathers often goes beyond issues relating to fatherhood or parenting. This broader scope acknowledges the complex social and personal contexts in which young fatherhood emerges. Practitioners tend to work through a range of issues over time, led directly by the specific support needs of the young father. For example, a young father's presenting issue might be getting access to his children, but over a six-month period he might be supported around topics such as basic skills and anger management, as well as getting advice on benefits and child development. One of the advantages of one-to-one work is that it provides a safe space to explore the bigger picture of young fathers' lives and experiences.

Practicalities: an ongoing approach

Mostly, one-to-one work is conducted in an open-ended way with the possibility of multiple contacts. Very few young fathers have just one session with a worker. Some workers have an open-door policy until the young men become too old for the service but this is subject to resources and funding issues. In our research (e.g. McDonnell et al., 2009; Sherriff, 2007), workers have commonly stressed the importance of a needs-led approach but also one that encourages ongoing contact that helps address clients' complex and changing issues.

One-to-one work happens in a range of locations such as young fathers' own homes, at school, in children's centres or in other programmes for young people. Sometimes workers go out with young fathers to other public places such as cafés or parks.

Fathers First Project: example of one-to-one working

Run in partnership with the Youth Service, local midwives, and the Connexions Service, Fathers First is connected with the Mobile Youth Initiative (MYI) which runs in isolated rural areas of the Isle of Wight. The MYI was aware that they were not reaching young fathers in rural areas. After consultation with agencies and young people, they realized that teenage fathers wanted one-to-one intensive support rather than group-based work. Consequently, holistic, flexible, and intensive individual support is now provided for young fathers, meeting them in an environment of their choice, or wherever they feel safe and comfortable.

> We meet young fathers wherever they feel safe or comfortable, it might be in their own home, at a park, whatever suits them – we travel to them.

One-to-one support is needs-led, starting from the young-fathers agenda. In the first instance, support usually relates to non-parenting issues (e.g. housing, employment, substance misuse, relationships, learning difficulties, legal issues etc.) but will move on to parenting support when the presenting issues have been dealt with. Support is wide-ranging and extensive.

> Individual support is totally led by the young father, we make sure he knows he will not be judged and that we are there for them – we look at the individual holistically and let them know that they can use our support for any area of their lives, not just parenting. It's them – we travel to them.

Key issues for reflection

- What struck you most about the information in the section on one-to-one work?
- Do you, or your organization, have the skills, knowledge and time to do one-to-one work? If not, how can you get them?

Group work with young fathers

Group work has the potential to provide different outcomes for young fathers compared with one-to-one work. A wider range of questions and issues can be explored by young fathers who each bring different perspectives and experiences, and have the chance to learn from each other. Group work has a strong history in work with young fathers in custody (see Lindfield, 2009).

One of the most exciting outcomes of group work with young fathers is that it can facilitate supportive relationships between participants: peer support and mentoring can be actively promoted by practitioners, or it can emerge informally as young fathers chat during group activities. In some groups, young fathers also attend with their children.

For younger and harder-to-reach fathers, developing a trusting relationship with a worker through one-to-one work normally precedes involvement in a group. It is worth noting that it can be harder to engage young fathers in group work than one-to-one work. The youngest fathers (e.g. school-age) are the least likely to get involved in group work, so most groups don't attract a full age range of young men.

Skills

Practitioners use a number of different strategies to make group work effective. Good facilitative and communication skills are essential, e.g. listening and letting young fathers know that they are important. Presenting information in an informal way can also work well. Practitioners work hard to make group work fun and hands-on. They need to be extremely flexible and adaptable around the content covered. Making sure everyone has a voice and is comfortable is not always easy, and meeting diverse needs can be hard. Some practitioners have considerable experience of running groups and knowledge of group-work theory and processes.

Issues covered in group work

The topics covered in group work are similar to those explored in one-to-one work, including practical parenting issues (such as preparing for labour, feeding your baby etc.), relationship issues (e.g. communicating with 'ex's') and building self-esteem and literacy skills. In less structured settings, group work can focus on the immediate issues and concerns of the young fathers present, e.g. the 'check-in' approach described below. Young fathers' groups invite other professionals in to work with participants around specific skills such as cooking and baby massage, or to provide information, such as on legal matters. Visiting professionals can also get a sense of the fathers' priorities when they do this. Some groups are set up for fathers to attend with their children – a space to just 'be', or to use messy play facilities.

Practicalities: resources and environment

In our research, practitioners tell us that group work with young fathers tends to take place in locations such as young people's projects, children's centres, libraries, leisure centres and other community settings. Practitioners have reported group numbers from 4–25 depending on the type of group. Longer-running groups tend to have smaller numbers attending each session (between 4–10), but rely on a larger pool of committed young fathers to attend, as not everyone comes each week. Group sessions last anything from 20 minutes to 3 hours and can be delivered on a weekly, monthly or on a more ad hoc basis. It is normal for group work to have fluctuating levels of interest from young fathers and some groups will dissolve and re-form regularly.

Stockport Specialist Midwives: example of group work

Two specialist midwives for young parents are employed by Stockport NHS Foundation Trust. Their remit is to look specifically at ways of reducing second pregnancies in teenage mothers as well as supporting young parents. As part of this work, young fathers are invited to attend a monthly Young Parents' Active Birth Workshop for young mothers and young fathers.

The aim of these young-parent-specific antenatal classes is to discuss issues around pregnancy, childbirth and parenting; to practise ways to help cope with labour and birth; to visit the delivery rooms; and to see the birth pools, and get the opportunity to ask questions in a relaxed, informal setting. The groups are small, with up to ten young women coming along with the young father-to-be/partner, mum or other supporter. As part of the session, time is allocated specifically for young fathers to get together informally to discuss their fears, concerns, excitement about the pregnancy, adapting to becoming a father, as well as their experiences of maternity services to-date. Following attendance at the first workshop, the prospective parents are then invited to attend a second session which looks at more specific issues around child care.

Key issues for reflection

- Do you or your organization have the knowledge, skills and time to provide group work support? If not, how can you get them?
- How can you ensure that the necessary one-to-one support is in place to make group work a success?
- What might prevent some young fathers from participating in groups?

Participatory approaches

In our research, we found that some practitioners wanted to involve young fathers in the delivery of projects in more structured and conscious ways, beyond the informal peer support that emerges from group work. This reflected particular views about how best to empower service users, as well as views on how to shape effective services. In our interviews, participatory approaches included: young fathers becoming peer mentors within a young-fathers group and encouraging new members to get involved and to feel welcome; young fathers running groups or co-facilitating groups on a range of issues relevant to parenting and beyond. Young fathers might also initiate, develop and prepare the content of sessions delivered to their peers.

Participatory approaches were seen as being located on a continuum where young fathers had more or less control over, and responsibility for, the projects they were involved in. Also, participatory approaches were seen as having their own momentum once they reached a critical mass. As young fathers became more involved, others wanted to follow suit and participation generated further participation. Of course, young people move on to new projects and interests so participatory approaches can also be fragile.

St Michael's Fellowship New Dad Project

This project in South London has been particularly successful in reaching young fathers from black and minority ethnic groups. It has found that involving young fathers as peer volunteers in delivering sessions, including those that are part of its antenatal input, has had an important impact on the young men the project is trying to reach because the volunteers can offer support that hits the spot:

> Peer working is really important as the volunteers (young fathers) have had similar experiences to those attending the project ... they may have just gone through the exact same thing ... the impact of this is far more profound and has a much stronger impact than we can as project workers (Project Co-ordinator).

Another example of the project's work is the Father Nature Project, which started as a short-term gardening project for fathers and children and is now exploring ways of becoming a fully autonomous social enterprise for the fathers involved.

Skills

Participatory approaches are underpinned by a variety of philosophies and aims including: empowerment of young people; skills development; and engaging communities in the issues that affect them. One practitioner we spoke to felt that it was sometimes easier to get young fathers involved in community issues than fatherhood issues initially, but that fathering skills improved as a consequence of community involvement.

Participatory approaches work best when the broader organization supported them (or could link them with existing volunteer schemes), as they can be time consuming and resource intensive in the start-up period.

Issues covered in participatory approaches

The issues covered within participatory approaches often mirrored those included in group work (see above). However, differences existed in how the groups were run and by whom. Topics covered included: safety awareness, cooking, baby care, play with children, breastfeeding as well as skills-building sessions around football, boxing, story-telling, gardening and self-defence.

Practicalities

In our research, practitioners agreed that young fathers had to meet certain criteria if they were going to be more involved in project delivery although those opportunities were open to all participants. The criteria included: having used the young-fathers project/s themselves; enthusiasm and energy for parenting issues and a child-focused approach; demonstrating a capacity for change; being flexible and adaptable; and having the capacity to work within broader organizational philosophies. Sometimes the young fathers involved in participatory approaches were a little older than the target group.

Young fathers involved in co-facilitation, mentoring or other types of volunteering received training in areas such as: child protection, basic health and safety, counselling, play work, confidentiality as well as undergoing other organizational induction processes. Generally young fathers' expenses such as travel costs were covered, and sometimes nominal payments were made for very regular work. In one organization, young fathers were paid normal casual rates when they did core organizational work. Young fathers were encouraged to apply for work within the organization where appropriate and their volunteering was often conceptualized as training. All young fathers involved in work with other young fathers were supervised by the relevant practitioners.

Mancroft Advice Project (MAP): an example of a participatory approach

MAP, located in Norwich is an independent information, advice and counselling service for young people aged between 11–25 years. Provision includes a drop-in for young fathers, practical advice and information, skills development, and support for issues relating to being young men as well as young fathers. Other services include advice on housing, benefits and advocacy, a children-and-young-people's rights worker, a young-fathers worker, free pregnancy testing, free condoms and a Connexions drop-in.

Two fathers who have used the Young Fathers Project at MAP for a number of years, regularly facilitate the weekly young-fathers group. They are supervised by the project manager, who is then able to do one-to-one work with clients during the group session time, if required. There has been a gradual and negotiated shift towards sharing responsibility for the running of the groups with the fathers. Initially, both fathers were involved in befriending new group members and informal peer support processes when they were young fathers. Participating in project delivery, as slightly older fathers, allows them a continuing connection to the project.

Key issues for reflection

- Are/could participatory approaches be part of your work? What might prevent this from happening?
- Discuss the material in this section with young people you work with. What are their views?

Challenges and ways forward

In this chapter, we have shown that work with young fathers is developing, but still not embedded in the work of universal services. How strong is the wave of change and how fragile are the achievements so far? These are key questions in the new 'age of austerity' as budget cuts on public services begin to bite. With no 'new money', will services revert back to the default position where young fathers are marginalized or will they continue to be acknowledged as central in work with children as services are reshaped by the new government? Certainly, the proposed expansion of health visiting offers potential for further engagement with young fathers (HM Government, 2010; Sherriff and Hall, 2011; Sherriff et al., 2009), as do plans to expand the Family Nurse Partnerships. The continued support for children's centres, including the focus on the more disadvantaged families should also benefit young families. However, as services are reshaped, key expertise is being lost as dedicated 'teenage pregnancy' posts are deleted. Staff training remains essential. The fear is that the progress achieved over the past decade or so might stall. However, we hope that the commitment of professionals leading this work will not allow the gains to be lost, and that slowly but surely, young fathers will continue to come out of the shadows and receive the support that will enable them to fulfil their desire to be the best fathers they can be for their children.

Conclusion

These issues have emerged as key features of successful approaches in work with young fathers:

- Having explicit values and aims that are rooted in notions of equality and empowerment.
- Adopting a range of approaches in order to reach and engage with young fathers. This involves maximizing relationships with young mothers, and forming stronger links with organizations that were reaching young men.
- Delivering support through a range of approaches with an emphasis on building rapport through one-to-one work. Youth work and counselling skills are valuable. Couples' work is also beginning to develop. Group work is a common method for working with young fathers, but take-up tends to be better following individual work.
- Young fathers themselves are beginning to play a role in the development and delivery of services, although this is generally a feature of more established projects which have a participatory ethos.

8

Working with Fathers of Disabled Children

Carol Potter and Kathy Rist

Introduction

There are around 770, 000 disabled children in the UK, the majority of whom live within their own nuclear families. A wide range of research suggests that families which include disabled children often have a range of needs and difficulties which are significantly different to those of families having no disabled children. Parents with disabled children experience much higher levels of stress, for example. However, much more is known in relation to the experiences of mothers of disabled children, as opposed to fathers (West, 2000). Fathers have often been seen as the 'invisible parent', being viewed largely as providers of support for their partners, rather than as parents in their own right, with their own range of issues. We know that such perceptions are ill-founded in general, with many fathers being deeply involved in caring for their disabled children.

This chapter will focus on the specific needs and experiences of fathers of disabled children, especially in the early years. To begin with, we will explore the extent to which fathers are involved in the care of their children before going on to discuss the needs and experiences of fathers, barriers to service inclusion and ways in which services can better support fathers of disabled children.

Fathers of disabled children: how involved are they?

Research has shown that there have been a number of barriers to father involvement in the care of their disabled children. These include working commitments, traditional expectations in relation to gender roles, the feminized nature of services, the timing of meetings and programmes which fathers could not attend and the fact that fathers have generally not been prepared for their parenting role but rather treated as an afterthought by services (Macdonald and Hastings, 2010). Having said this, several studies have shown that fathers are highly involved in the care of their disabled children. For example, Towers (2009) conducted an in-depth survey of 251 fathers of children with learning disabilities, finding that men were highly involved in providing care for their children, often rearranging working commitments in order to do this. The survey also found that most men wanted to spend more time with their children, being prevented from doing so by work obligations. This is one of the largest studies in recent years to focus on the needs and challenges experienced by fathers of disabled children. This study also found that fathers thought it especially important to develop a caring relationship with their children through involvement in leisure activities and by actively supporting their children in their education and learning. Towers (2009) concluded that fathers, in particular, may play a key role in supporting the development of communication strategies and programmes for children with disabilities.

Needs and difficulties

Experiences of parenting a disabled child: differences between mothers and fathers

We know that mothers and fathers have many experiences in common, in relation to parenting a disabled child. For example, both parents are more likely to experience higher levels of stress than parents of non-disabled children for a variety of reasons, including managing gender roles; parents not having enough time to spend together; dealing with grief after the birth of a disabled child; coping with the child's different development path and dealing with significant financial difficulties (Glenn, 2007). Lack of access to services is another key stressor, with a survey by Mencap (2006) noting that 70% of families containing at least one child with learning disabilities have reached, or have almost reached breaking point due to lack of service provision. It is, however, becoming increasingly clear that mothers and fathers experience parenting a disabled child in different ways, leading to different sets of needs. Traditionally, it has most often been the experiences and needs of mothers which have been best understood and addressed by support services, with fathers' needs largely going unmet (SCIE, 2005) which has important and potentially detrimental effects on the whole family.

The Social Care Institute for Excellence (2005) in a literature review on the subject, emphasized that fathers of disabled children are fathers first, and as such share many of the same experiences as other fathers. Like other men, they place a significant importance on being a father and find the role a positive and valuable one (Carpenter, 2002). However, they are more likely to be stressed than fathers of non-disabled children and the issues which cause them stress are likely to differ in some ways from issues which promote stress in mothers of disabled children. For example, fathers are more likely than mothers to be stressed by their child's general behaviour and disposition, by their own ability to bond with their child and by their ability to provide for their child's future (Pelchat et al., 2003). Such findings have implications for service responses to men. For example, it may be especially important to ensure that fathers have the same access as mothers to training on behaviour management.

Below, we will explore the range of needs and issues which relate specifically to fathers of disabled children in more detail.

Emotional responses: the diagnosis and early years

Studies have shown that fathers often experience intense emotional reactions to the birth of a disabled child (Hornby, 1992; West, 2000) and that these reactions largely go unnoticed and unsupported. Hornby's (1992) analysis of eight fathers' accounts of becoming the father of a disabled child highlighted the deep and conflicting emotions which men experienced, both positive and challenging, together with the personal growth which occurred during this difficult period. Such themes emerged more recently in Towers' research, involving 251 fathers of children with learning disabilities. One father reflecting on his disabled daughter's early years said:

> Looking back, I know now that I was just about functioning for the first three years of my daughter's life. I had suffered a huge blow (along with my wife) and we spiralled into a very deep depression. All of our friends were pushed away and our families began to distance themselves as we increasingly struggled to cope ... I continued to go to work, it was the only stable thing in my life. But the work I did was low paid and demanded a lot from me. I kept my home life private from my friends and colleagues, unable to join in with the conversations about their kids. I was angry, sad and resentful of their 'normal' children they so readily bragged about (Towers, 2009, p. iv).

Access to information

One of the key early and ongoing difficulties for parents is getting access to timely, accurate and accessible information. Following the birth of a disabled child, parents have so many questions, as highlighted by one father who said:

> You need to talk to someone because we are entering a big world now that is going to affect the rest of your lives and you need someone to tell you what happens, what are you entitled to, what can you do, what can't you do, what should I do, what do you think? Give me your experiences. Because you are opening the door of something that is just well, unreal. When you start off it just overwhelms you, totally overwhelms you ... (Harrison et al., p. 21).

The SCIE report (2005) suggested that fathers are especially concerned about getting information both in relation to their child's difficulties and the services available for the child and the family. This is especially the case immediately following diagnosis. Father concerns have been shown to change over time, with issues regarding information on the child's disability and services diminishing gradually, as worries for the child's future begin to grow. Most parents of disabled children find access to benefits and necessary equipment a struggle to a greater or lesser extent. One father said of his experience:

> It's so difficult to get what you want in the disabled world. It's all fight, fight fight. If you don't use and contact the right people, then no-one will tell you (Harrison, Henderson and Leonard, 2007, p. 73).

It can often be the case that fathers are given the role of pressing for equipment or resources, which brings fathers into contact with services possibly for the first time, as we shall see next.

Contact with services

The strong perception of many fathers of disabled children is that services are generally geared to supporting mothers rather than fathers, as is the case for other men. Fathers do not feel included in services for a number of reasons. These may range from the timings of meetings which take place while fathers are working, to the attitudes and beliefs of professionals who may acknowledge the father's contribution and may therefore exclude him from discussions and decision-making. Over 100 fathers of children with learning disabilities, for example, reported that they were not sufficiently involved at the time of their child's diagnosis which left them feeling excluded, right at the start, when trying to deal with extremely difficult news (Towers, 2009). Men felt that there was not enough opportunity for informal contact with professionals which would have been especially useful since formal meetings often take place during the working day. Towers (2009) argues that such a lack of informal contact may well have an impact on fathers' confidence in supporting their child, especially if they feel nervous during more formal meetings. This may be particularly the case for fathers with lower educational qualifications. Such a situation may well then affect the relationship of the father with his child for some time to come.

One professional, very experienced in working with families of disabled children spoke about the way in which professionals may convey under-mining messages regarding fathers' roles, responsibilities and competence:

> First of all, fathers are not seen as the primary carer of their child, most things go through mothers ... I've worked with single fathers of disabled children and still our society is looking for a female figure in that child's life ... in meetings there are always questions about who cares for this child ... who is doing the day to day caring? And that is seen to be women's work ... and that is disempowering for the man ... because the message he is getting immediately is ... you don't know how to do this ... (Personal communication, 2011).

Such attitudes spring from a deficit model of fatherhood which was discussed in Chapter 1. It may be that such views of men as not being sufficiently capable of caring for their children are especially prevalent where children are disabled and are seen as needing special kinds of care. Such attitudes, if conveyed to fathers, may clearly serve to undermine their confidence in caring for their disabled children.

Father attitudes: a potential barrier?

It may not only be a question of the attitudes of services though. Fathers also may bring a range of challenging attitudes with them when first encountering services. An expert in the field of working with families with disabled children noted that fathers are often called in by their partners to 'fix a problem' in relation to service provision and the men's attitude to services may well be significantly influenced by their partners' previous experiences. In such situations, fathers may therefore appear to professionals as adversarial and challenging. A key approach for practitioners in such circumstances is to recognize the difficulties and stresses which families with disabled children face on a daily basis and to convey to fathers, in explicit ways, that their voices are being heard and that the process is inclusive of them.

Employment and financial concerns

Moving on to wider issues, with regard to employment, fathers of disabled children have reported that they make significant changes to their working patterns (Towers, 2009). In particular, fathers tend to seek employment where there is the opportunity for more flexible working patterns, to allow them to meet their family commitments, often at the expense of promotion and increased salary. Most fathers said that they could discuss their family situation with employers but some could not. More than half the fathers surveyed did not know that they could request flexible working, with only 37 out of 251 having done so. Furthermore, three-quarters of fathers did not know that they were entitled to unpaid leave (Towers, 2009).

Related to issues of employment, fathers seem especially concerned about the financial implications of having a disabled child which often leads to loss of income from mothers, increased cost in areas of transport and home adaptations. Families with disabled children are much more at risk of living in poverty for a range of reasons, including the inability of both parents to work due to caring responsibilities and the significantly increased cost of bringing up a disabled child which is not sufficiently addressed by the benefits system (SCIE, 2005).

Impact on fathers' health

As a result of the difficulties outlined above, mothers and fathers experience higher levels of stress than parents of non-disabled children. In the Towers research (2009), fathers of children with learning disabilities said that they experienced stress nearly half of the time. Half of the men surveyed also felt that their physical health was also being affected and that they received very little help in coping with this.

Concern about the future

As we have already discussed above, what will happen in the future to their disabled children when they are no longer there to care for them is a major concern for all mothers and fathers of disabled children, and this issue is one that services need to address explicitly with both parents.

Lack of sources of emotional support

Given the range of difficulties experienced by fathers of disabled children, it is of concern to note that most tend to have few sources of emotional support, largely relying on their partner for this. Peer support from friends with typically developing children seems difficult to come by, as one father of a child with autism reflected:

> Talking about your own circumstances with your mates is boring. I have seen friends glaze over if I talk about my child (Harrison, Henderson and Leonard, 2007).

Another father with sole care of a child with muscular dystrophy talked about the lack of peer support due to both lack of time and resources:

> I don't have many friends. I haven't got time for friends … I have very little social life … I had a huge amount of friends but they just dropped off one by one because I don't have the time to phone them or keep in contact. The bairn comes first – not my friends (Harrison, Henderson and Leonard, 2007).

Most fathers in Towers' (2009) survey said that they would value somebody outside the family to share concerns with. This was a theme which also emerged from West's study of four fathers.

> I needed someone to say, come on [Dan] it is OK, come and sit down for five minutes or to be taken outside for half an hour and said I'll see you in a bit and

I'll have a chat about it, think about what questions you want to ask, come back in and we will talk about it. We can talk about what next … I needed information and I needed somebody to talk to, other than family members … I really did need someone to talk to … I needed an external, somebody different, it wouldn't have mattered what race, colour, creed or gender it was. Somebody that I could sit down with and say 'look I'm having a really bad time, I'm really worried about the future, am I doing this right, is it my fault?' I needed someone just to analyse the baggage out of it. I really did need it …' (West, 2000, p. 17).

Impact on family dynamics

The wide range of pressures on mothers and fathers can, and often do, have a negative impact on couples' relationships, with parents of disabled children being at much greater risk of marital difficulties and divorce. The Towers (2009) survey of 251 fathers of disabled children found that men felt that they did not have enough time to spend with their partners due to the demands of caring for a disabled child. Fathers also felt guilty and pressurized because they felt that they were not spending enough time with their non-disabled children. In a review of the literature on family dynamics in families with disabled children, Glenn (2007) suggested that where families were not provided with sufficient support to address their difficulties, a complex negative cycle of interactions within the family was likely to develop, with fathers possibly withdrawing from aspects of family life, mothers feeling increasingly unsupported, leading to conflict between parents which may increase children's challenging behaviour which in turn leads to greater tension within the household, sometimes resulting in a breakdown of the parents' relationship and subsequently divorce. Such a damaging cycle of events has negative impacts on all of those involved, especially children. We know that children in households where there is conflict between parents are likely to suffer poorer health and to be at an increased risk of psychological problems later on (see Jekielek, 1998, for example). Conversely, higher levels of father involvement with their disabled children has been found to be positively associated with a harmonious relationship with their partner (Pleck and Masciadrelli, 2004). It is therefore clear that supporting the relationship of parents of disabled children is one of the most important ways of maintaining a stable family life, as we shall explore below.

We have seen that fathers experience a range of difficulties, some of which are different from those experienced by mothers of disabled children and that these difficulties often go largely unaddressed by services. If the significant needs of mothers and fathers go unmet, there is a significant risk of conflict and breakdown within the couple's relationship which clearly has negative repercussions for the whole family and especially children.

A number of approaches have been identified which practitioners can adopt to better include fathers in a range of family services, thereby better supporting them, in what is often an extremely challenging parenting role.

Key strategies for father inclusion

Acknowledging the father's role

We have discussed the extent to which fathers are actively involved in the care of their disabled children, while also providing vital emotional support for their partners. It is also clear that their role in relation to their child is very often not sufficiently recognized by a range of services with which they come into contact. Towers (2009) asked 251 fathers of children with learning disabilities what was the best thing that services could do for them as fathers. The most common reply was the need for recognition as fathers, who should be accorded the same respect as mothers and who should be equally involved in discussions and decision-making:

> Explicitly acknowledge that as a father my responses might be different from the responses of my wife (Towers, 2009, p.167).

A father in West's study (2000) made a similarly powerful argument:

> To be actively involved, to be asked questions and when questions are asked, direct them at me … recognizing the fact that the father's role is just as important as the mother's role and that I do take an active part (West, 2000, p. 21).

Such an approach may require a significant shift in staff perceptions and the ethos and delivery of services. Staff may need to consider their own attitudes and beliefs about the involvement of fathers in order to assess how approaches to better supporting fathers may be improved.

Key issues for reflection

- Try to consider objectively any recent interactions with mothers and fathers of disabled children which you have had.
- What were your expectations of each parent in relation to the care of their child?
- To what extent were both parents actively encouraged to be involved in decision-making relating to their child?

Having considered the need to adopt a positive ethos in relation to fathers of disabled children, we will move on to consider how services can best support men during key stages of their child's early life.

Support at the time of diagnosis

As we have seen above, the diagnosis of a child with a disability and the months afterwards constitute an extremely stressful time for both mothers and fathers. It is vitally important that both parents are supported through this very difficult time. SENSE, the charity for deaf-blind children, emphasized the need for both parents to be present at the diagnosis, otherwise one parent, usually the mother, may become the 'bearer of bad news'. Mary Guest (SENSE, 2001), an expert in the field, commented that when both parents are present at the diagnosis, there is immediately common ground and opportunity to share the initial shock and grief and ask questions which can be extremely strengthening for couples. There is also an opportunity for professionals to offer support to both parents at this very early stage.

A study by Beresford and colleagues (2007) asked mothers and fathers of disabled children what they would most like services to do to support them. One of the key issues to emerge was that both parents thought that services needed to do much more to support fathers' emotional needs and especially their adjustment to their child's initial diagnosis. If fathers are not supported at this extremely difficult stage, then this is likely to have an undermining effect on their ability to cope and become involved, as one father highlighted above. Similarly, fathers interviewed in a study by the Foundation for People with Learning Disabilities (2007), thought that the provision of counselling soon after diagnosis would be helpful for mothers and fathers.

Key issues for reflection

- To what extent does your service ensure that both mothers and fathers are present when a diagnosis is given?
- To what extent does your service offer support to both mothers and fathers following diagnosis?
- How might these aspects of the service be improved?

The PRIFAM (Programme for Family Intervention) approach, developed in Canada (Pelchat and Lefebvre, 2004) has been structured to be effective in supporting parents during the first 6 months after their child's diagnosis. The programme consists of 6 to 8 meetings between a nurse and both parents, during which the nurse focuses on developing positive beliefs and developing coping strategies. The programme is wholly inclusive of fathers since it emphasizes the need to support each parent as an individual, as a part of a couple and as a parent. It begins from the moment a diagnosis is made, so that support is available to both parents from the start. A key element of the programme is that each parent is encouraged to acknowledge their response to the diagnosis, seen as an important step in moving forward in adapting to their altered situation. This step ensures that fathers are always given the opportunity to discuss their initial response, which, as we have seen, is often not the case. Finally, there is an emphasis on each person in the family developing their own skills and resources which again is empowering for men whose possible contribution is often much less considered. Programme developers emphasize that the success of the programme is based on the growth of a trusting relationship between the nurse and both parents. Again, this allows for the development of a source of support for the father as well as the mother from an early stage. The PRIFAM model appears to have much to offer in terms of providing an early and empowering approach to supporting both fathers and mothers of disabled children.

Key issues for reflection

- Are there aspects of this model which could be introduced within your service?
- How might this be achieved? What would be the first step?

Ongoing provision of advice and guidance

As time goes on, both mothers and fathers will continue to need access to a wide range of professional advice and guidance since their child's developmental path may be significantly different to that of non-disabled children, in important ways. It is therefore essential that both parents are included in all sessions where professionals are providing guidance on how best to support their child's development. Where only mothers are present, this can lead to poorer outcomes for children. West (2000) reports the responses of two fathers who had been included during the visits of two specialist practitioners:

> A pre-school teacher that came when he was only months old. I thought it was really good she just came to sort of teach us really and showing us how to stimulate him and using bright colours and what have you (West, 2000, p. 19).

> ... we had another change of speech therapist and the new girl was brilliant. She couldn't do enough for us, she came round to the house, she told us what to get and she supplied the flashcards and she told us to get this and get that ... she was the only one like spoke to me as a parent rather than as a male or female. It was a parent. (West, 2000, p. 19).

Contact a Family, a national organization (http://www.cafamily.org.uk) , has been working with mothers and fathers of disabled children for over 30 years and have suggested a number of important steps which professionals across the disciplines can take to better include men. These are contained within a very useful booklet: 'Fathers', available free online at http://www.cafamily.org.uk/pdfs/fathers.pdf . A summary of the approaches suggested are provided below.

Including fathers in meetings

Parents of disabled children will have to attend a large number of meetings with a range of professionals during the course of their child's life. Meetings should be arranged when both parents can attend. Professionals should start from the assumption that fathers are actively involved in the care of their disabled child. They should make a conscious effort to talk to both parents at every meeting. Both mothers and fathers should be encouraged to ask questions during meetings. If the father cannot attend a meeting, for whatever reason, professionals should make sure that they contact the father afterwards by phone to ensure that he is involved in the process and that he receives any relevant written information, rather than expecting that this will be passed on through the mother.

It is also important to ensure that information is sent to both resident and non-resident fathers. Due to the demands of having a disabled child, there is a high level of separation and divorce among parents, as stated above and therefore including non-resident fathers is a particular issue for services working with disabled children and their families. (See Chapter 10 for more information on working with separated fathers).

One health visitor talked about her efforts to involve fathers in her work:

> What I have tried to do in the past ... is to involve the dads. I rarely meet the dads. There is one who is keen to talk to me, and I try to organize my visits to fit in with his shift work. A way of overcoming this problem for the others is to try to leave something with the parents, even just a sheet of paper, that they could talk about. I try to make clips of video that the parents could look at together and try to discuss their ideas (Jones and Ware, 1997, p. 6).

Schools need also to take account of the need to arrange meetings at a time when fathers can attend. As a former teacher of children with autism, the first author routinely arranged meetings with parents at their own home in the evenings, thus ensuring fathers were kept fully informed of their children's progress at school, as well as being able to share their concerns or ask questions.

West (2000) provides the response of one father who felt that he had been fully included in a meeting with his child's paediatrician:

> I think the most helpful thing has been the positive attitude of the paediatrician. As I say we saw him on a six monthly cycle basis when he was first born and then after that on an annual basis. He would ask us how he was doing and we would tell him and he would keep saying 'is there anything else you need?' and he put into motion anything we thought we needed ... He seemed to have a lot of time for us and a lot of time for Ben (West, 2000, p.18).

Key issues for reflection

- To what extent does your service ensure that meetings take place when fathers can attend?
- What steps could be taken to move towards both greater father inclusion in meetings or to contact fathers if they cannot attend?

Supporting the couple's relationship

Since, as we have seen, the relationship of many couples with a disabled child is likely to come under significant strain, services need to consider how best they can support that relationship. The use of counselling has been shown to be helpful to both partners in resolving issues associated with stress and conflict by developing more effective means of communication (Seligman and Darling, 2007).

The provision of timely respite care is also considered a major source of support for a couple's relationship, providing that this is what parents want and is of a high quality. Unfortunately, such care is in short supply, with The Parliamentary Hearings on Services for Disabled Children (2006) reporting that the lack of short breaks was the biggest single cause of dissatisfaction with service provision.

Offering access to peer support

Some fathers have shown a preference for receiving support from other fathers of disabled children, although this may not be the way forward for everyone (SCIE, 2008). It is important to address the stated individual preferences of men. Contact with other fathers avoids the potentially painful experience of comparing their own child's skills and abilities with those of typically developing children. Contact a Family highlights the fact that such groups need not consist of only talking about their difficulties, which may be problematic for some men but might also take a more active format, focusing on taking part in activities with their children.

Stepfathers

Services need to bear in mind that stepfathers will need as much information and support as biological fathers, coming into a family and taking responsibility for a disabled child.

Challenges and ways forward

As Nigel Sherriff and colleagues discussed in Chapter 7, at the time of writing, public services in the UK face challenging times with significant cuts to budgets ahead. There are realistic fears that benefits to families with a disabled child could be significantly affected, as well as support services. In such a climate, it is especially important for services to offer support to mothers and fathers of disabled children as this may represent one of the most effective ways of keeping families together. It is time for fathers to become visible parents at every point in the service-provision process, during the antenatal period, the traumatic period of diagnosis and beyond.

Summary

- Mothers and fathers share a number of experiences in parenting a disabled child but may also differ in their responses to the challenges of such parenting in important ways.
- Much more is known about the needs of mothers of disabled children than fathers.
- Fathers of disabled children have a range of needs which largely go unmet.
- Key approaches for practitioners in supporting fathers of disabled children are to:
  - recognize the father's needs and role explicitly
  - actively engage fathers in decision-making
  - seek to include the father in meetings which will take place
  - offer informal contact where fathers are unable to attend meetings

- ensure that fathers are able to access all advice and guidance sessions on supporting their child's development
- seek to support the couple's relationship, especially through the provision of respite services
- offer access to peer support.

9

Working with Fathers from Minority Ethnic Backgrounds

Roger Olley

Chapter Outline

Introduction

This chapter will explore issues regarding the engagement of fathers from minority ethnic communities and will develop 'good practice points' for practitioners seeking to be inclusive in their service delivery.

As we have seen, there are a significant number of studies on the important part that fathers play in the lives of children and families but relatively little is known, by researchers and policy-makers, about fathering among black and minority ethnic populations in the UK. Of those studies that have been undertaken, a significant proportion have low numbers of participants so care must be taken when considering their conclusions as they may not be representative. These studies do, however, give practitioners a glimpse into some of the experiences and challenges that fathers from a wide variety of cultural backgrounds may encounter. Generally, the take-up of family-support services by minority ethnic groups is lower than that of other families. The Department of Health and Social Service's Inspectorate document *Excellence Not Excuses*

(2000) reported that most local authorities had not developed adequate approaches to delivering accessible services to minority ethnic communities. Page and colleagues (2007), found that nearly all of the local authorities in their research found engaging with fathers much more challenging than working with mothers. As we have examined throughout this book, there is overwhelming evidence that father involvement significantly affects child outcomes. Therefore service engagement with both parents from all ethnic backgrounds is essential.

> ### Key issues for reflection
>
> - To what extent is your service engaging families from minority ethnic communities?
> - To what extent is your service engaging fathers from minority ethnic communities?

Barriers to service use

There are a number of barriers which serve to make services less accessible to mothers and fathers from minority ethnic backgrounds, which we will examine in this section.

Low income

Page and colleagues (2007) noted that barriers such as cost, distance to services, and lack of time may affect all parents, but argued that parents from minority ethnic backgrounds are more likely to be poorer and therefore disproportionately disadvantaged. For example, the Equal Opportunities Commission (2007) reported that two in five Bangladeshi and Pakistani families were living on low incomes.

Language and communication issues

Language and communication difficulties may create significant barriers to service use for both mothers and fathers from some minority ethnic backgrounds, both in terms of understanding what services are available and in the actual use of those services (Page and colleagues, 2007).

Cultural beliefs and practices in relation to fathering

There are a number of cultural issues which need to be taken into account regarding attitudes to the father's role in family life within minority ethnic communities. A Department of Health (2010) report on the views of parents from minority ethnic communities on the parenting journey in early childhood found that cultural influences were likely to affect fathers' attitudes to pregnancy, preparing for the child's birth, and engaging with health services. The report outlined some of the issues that should be borne in mind when trying to involve fathers from minority ethnic communities in antenatal and post-natal activities. For example, fathers from Gypsy and Traveller communities invariably adopted the role of the provider, often working away from home with relatively little involvement in the pregnancy. Women in these communities had strong female support networks during pregnancy and appeared to require little male support. The report concluded that: 'Not only are men unlikely to want to be involved, the women are also very unlikely to encourage them' (p. 45). In relation to Pakistani parents, the report found that there was significant cultural sensitivity surrounding pregnancy, with fathers avoiding antenatal classes to avoid seeing other pregnant women and women themselves reluctant to attend to avoid being seen.

Both examples pose significant challenges for agencies who are reaching out to these communities. Services working with Gypsy and Traveller communities may need to shift the emphasis of their father involvement work to a later period in the children's lives. Those wishing to involve Pakistani fathers in antenatal classes may need to develop ways of working that involve, for example, separate classes for men and women.

Insufficient recognition of both similarity and diversity

A major pitfall for service providers to avoid is a tendency to 'homogenize' the experience of mothers and fathers from minority ethnic backgrounds. There are both similarities and differences between majority and minority ethnic groups in relation to fatherhood. For example, Salway, Chowbey and Clarke's (2009) study of Asian fathers found that they had much in common with fathers from other UK ethnic groups, including white fathers. A key issue to bear in mind is that regardless of race, ethnicity or culture, fathers want the best for their children and are ambitious for them. Razwan (2006), in a small-scale study of 23 British Bangladeshi and Pakistani fathers (87% of whom were born outside the UK) found all with high aspirations for their children's educational achievement. Salway, Chowbey and Clarke (2009) argued that:

> There is therefore a need to challenge the 'othering' and homogenising of minority ethnic fathers that can occur through the design of services and the attitudes of practitioners (p. 7).

It is equally important to recognize difference where it does exist, to understand that there may be significant cultural variations between social and ethnic groups. For example, the term 'Chinese community' is often used to refer to people from Hong Kong, Singapore, Taiwan and Malaysia. Such a stance exemplifies cultural insensitivity since there is as much diversity in languages, parenting practices, attitudes and beliefs within this 'community'. Of course, the individuality of the fathers that services are seeking to engage with always needs to be recognized along with the fact that individuals often face multiple disadvantage, so an individual's ethnic group should never be seen in isolation.

Atkin and Chattoo (2007) observed that the challenge for family support services is to develop:

> a reflexive practice, enabling professionals to respond to the needs of people from minority ethnic populations without recourse to homogenized notions of culture, religion or community (p. 393).

There is also a need to understand and respond to significant feelings of anxiety in relation to wider community participation. Khan (2006) in his study of 26 Muslim fathers found that most British Muslim fathers are keen to integrate but cautious of the perceived Islamophobic attitude of wider society to Islam and Muslims, often incited by the media.

Agencies, therefore need to avoid basing service development on the basis of the cultural background of the majority ethnic group which may not be relevant or acceptable to potential service users. Barn, Ladino and Brooke (2006) concluded in their report *Parenting in Multi-racial Britain* that:

> The heterogeneity of minority ethnic family life is complex and needs to be understood in the context of migration, ethnicity, socio-economic circumstances, multiculturalism, and racism (p. 1).

Negative experiences of service use

In their 2006 paper, *Young Black Fathers and Maternity Services*, Pollock et al. observed that although none of the fathers identified ethnicity as a barrier to service use, it is important to take account of the impact of a 'quadruple identity', that is, being black, young, male and generally poor. They argue that:

> Young Black men's expectations may be so reduced because of past experiences in the educational and employment systems that they may not expect to be involved or do not know what they need to know (p. 3).

Non-resident fathers

The issue of delivering services to fathers from some minority ethnic backgrounds can be complicated by patterns of residence. Hunt and Platt (2009) reported that Black British fathers are twice as likely as White British fathers (and three times as likely as British Asian fathers) to live apart from their children. High rates of non-resident fathers are also found where children are of mixed heritage. The implications for services are twofold. First, it is vital not to make the assumption that non-resident fathers will be less involved in their children's lives and second, that the pattern of service delivery needs to take account of non-residence in terms of when, where and how services are delivered to fathers.

Key issues for reflection

Consider each of the barriers above:
- To what extent does your service recognize these challenges?
- In each area, in what ways does your service attempt to overcome such barriers?

Developmental and legal imperatives

Father involvement and child outcomes

We have seen that there are a range of significant barriers to the inclusion of fathers from minority ethnic backgrounds in family support services, despite the very strong arguments for doing so. We have explored the many benefits of positive father involvement in relation to child outcomes in Chapter 1. In 2010, the then Department for Children, Schools and Families stated in their *Think Family* guidance:

> Research shows that children with highly involved fathers develop better friend-
> ships and more empathy, have higher levels of educational achievement and
> self-esteem, and are less likely to become involved with crime or substance abuse.
> At the same time, mothers also benefit greatly from the support that fathers
> can provide, particularly in helping to balance work-life commitments (p. 15,
> para. 43).

The Healthy Child Programme (2009) reinforces the importance of fathers:

> The contribution that fathers make to their children's development, health and
> well-being is important, but services do not do enough to recognize or support
> them. Research shows that a father's behaviour, beliefs and aspirations can
> profoundly influence the health and well-being of both mother and child in
> positive and negative ways (p. 11).

Fathers play a crucial part in determining and shaping their children's
futures and early years practitioners, seeking to be more effective in their
work, should tailor their services to meet the needs of all fathers by sensitive
involvement with relevant aspects of their race, culture and beliefs.

Legal frameworks

There is also a legal imperative which we shall discuss here. The Race
Relations Act 1976, updated through the Race Relations (Amendment) Act
2000, outlawed discrimination by any public body on racial grounds (directly,
indirectly or by victimization) and placed a positive duty on all public bodies
to tackle institutional racism. Institutional racism was described in the 1999
MacPherson Report as:

> The collective failure of an organization to provide an appropriate and profes-
> sional service to people because of their colour, culture or ethnic origin. It can
> be seen or detected in processes, attitudes and behaviour which amount to
> discrimination through unwitting prejudice, ignorance, thoughtlessness and
> racist stereotyping which disadvantage minority ethnic people (p. 34).

This definition acknowledges that individual practitioners working within
agencies may not be racially prejudiced themselves but that racism can still
be inherent in the systematic operation of the institution.

The law demands inclusion through the Gender Equality Duty (2007) and
the Race Relations Amendment Act (2000). Since April 2001, local authorities
have been subject to an enforceable 'General Duty' under the Act. This duty
states that in carrying out all their functions, public authorities must have
due regard to the need to eliminate unlawful racial discrimination, promote

equality of opportunities and to promote good race relations. It is now incumbent upon service providers to demonstrate that they treat different groups fairly, challenge discrimination and promote inter-group harmony.

It is important that health and social care providers recognize that individual parents have different requirements rather than offering one standard of service for everyone. The need to reduce inequity and improve access to health and social care for minority ethnic communities has been recognized and commented upon over the years. The Acheson Inquiry (1998), which was key in putting health inequalities onto the political agenda, recommended that policies needed to consider, and be sensitive to, the needs of minority ethnic groups in service provision and health care. The Darzi Report (2007) also proposed a remedy for health inequalities by making services more accessible to people from all communities.

Key issue for reflection

- Does your agency actively promote equality of opportunity for fathers from minority ethnic backgrounds? If so, how?

Including fathers from minority ethnic backgrounds: approaches

We saw in Chapter 4 that maternity and child-health services have difficulties engaging with fathers generally, so managing additional issues, such as those around issues of ethnicity and culture, can seem particularly daunting. Here we will examine methods of approaching these issues in practice.

Understanding the importance of working with fathers

We have seen that it is important that early years teams develop a 'corporate view' of fathers and what they are trying to achieve. As discussed earlier, every practitioner in a team has a highly personal experience of being fathered or not being fathered and it is evident that this personal experience may impact on the way that they work. A move from an individualistic to a reflective, research-based 'corporate view' will make teams more effective in working with all fathers to enable positive outcomes for their children. Such a position is fundamental to fathers work. Once this is established then agencies can begin to understand and address issues of diversity within fatherhood.

Acknowledging complex experience

When developing early years work with the fathers in families from minority ethnic backgrounds, experiences of migration, ethnicity, socio-economic circumstances, multiculturalism and racism need to be acknowledged and validated. If this validation and acknowledgement does not occur, it may lead to poor service development which will lead to poor service delivery and, consequently, poor service uptake by the fathers.

Raising staff awareness

It will be vital to raise awareness of issues relevant to fathers from differing minority ethnic backgrounds. The small numbers of research studies that are available do reveal that fathers often differ across cultures as to how they understand, define, and practise 'active fatherhood'. If practitioners do not understand and recognize that these differences exist then this can lead them to assume that the model for involved fathering is middle class, educated and Western. We have seen that in Khan's (2006) discussions with 26 Muslim fathers, these men felt cautious about engaging with the dominant culture due to their perception that wider community attitudes to Islam could be challenging. Work by the Equal Opportunities Commission (EOC) (2007) found that fathers from ethnic minority groups were less likely to feel confident about their capacity to care for their children and more likely to perceive their role in the family as being primarily about earning a wage. Staff attempting to engage with fathers from this background need to be highly sensitive to such issues, if they are to work effectively with them, drawing out the advantages of a more involved role for fathers without minimizing their role as providers.

A holistic approach

From their review of a number of case studies of services successful in engaging families from black and minority ethnic communities, Page and colleagues (2007) concluded that a holistic approach to family needs worked most effectively. A concern with a wider range of family needs was important in developing strong relationships with staff delivering services.

Consultation with members of minority ethnic communities

The development of relevant and achievable goals should be significantly enhanced through a process of ongoing consultation with mothers and fathers from minority ethnic backgrounds. The establishment of such a process is likely to take time and effort, with a dedicated worker, in whom the local community can trust, generally being a prerequisite. Page and colleagues (2007) detailed the process of engaging Bangladeshi parents in the local Coram Parents' Centre in the Kings Cross area of London. When the Community Development worker was asked why she thought the Centre was not engaging members of the Bangladeshi community at the time she was recruited, she said that the Centre was not dealing with the community's own issues: 'You have to deal with people's priorities and then draw people in' (p. 34).

If the views and requirements of both parents are taken into account in service development, there is a much greater likelihood that these services will then be taken up.

Developing trust: recruiting staff from local communities

The development of trusting relationships with staff are vital in any service. However, they are particularly important when working with people who, for a variety of reasons have not engaged with services before. Again, from the study by Page and colleagues (2007), one Bangladeshi mother said:

> the staff are key – when they are like family members, it really doesn't matter who runs the service (p. 35).

One of the strategies which was found to be effective in developing trust across the case studies was the recruitment of staff from local communities, which helped to reduce a feeling of 'them and us', although staff were not necessarily ethnically matched to communities with whom they would be working.

Making contact with faith groups

Engaging with faith groups is important. By involving the leaders of these groups, it may be possible to gain access to opportunities to communicate and consult with large numbers of fathers in an effective way. It is vitally important that practitioners gain an understanding at a very early stage, of how faith informs, guides and supports fatherhood in different communities. By gaining such an understanding, effective and meaningful ways of working can be developed.

Working with mothers

As we have seen in relation to fathers generally, involving mothers to inform and help teams involve fathers is a useful way of progressing the work in ways that are meaningful and pertinent to the target group. Mothers are vitally important in this context in that they can communicate and reach out to the fathers the service is seeking to engage.

Having a realistic action plan and timetable

Engaging fathers can be a challenging exercise for services and, as we have discussed, there will be additional issues to consider when working with fathers from minority ethnic backgrounds. It is therefore essential for effective working to develop realistic plans that all team members subscribe to and which lays out their tasks and responsibilities. The plan will lead to an understanding of **Who** will do it? **What** will they be doing? **Where** will it be done? **When** will it be done? **How** will it be done?

Key issues for reflection

- What areas of training are needed to enhance the work of your agency for working with fathers from minority ethnic communities?
- Are there any structural changes that need to be made in your organization to improve work with minority ethnic fathers?
- What changes could you make quickly to begin the process of engaging more fathers?

Conclusion

It is recognized that inequalities in employment, housing and education can adversely affect the inclusion of many in our society. However, the additional pressures of migration, cultural differences, experiences of racism, lack of extended family and community support, individuals' lack of a sense of identity and belonging, and of course communication barriers, also need to be recognized and addressed. Services need to understand diversity in fatherhood which includes differences in race, religion and cultural beliefs. Inclusive provision inevitably develops from an in-depth understanding of the culture, history and individual experiences and needs of those who have previously been excluded. Consultation with mothers and fathers is therefore essential, together with a willingness to act on feedback given. The development of trusting relationships is also key and can be enhanced by recruiting staff from local communities and working closely with faith leaders and other community leaders. Much remains to be done in this key area but there are examples of good practice which others can build upon.

10

Working with Separated Fathers

Geoff Read

Chapter Outline

Introduction

This chapter will explore a number of key issues in relation to separated fathers, beginning with some facts and figures and going on to explore why it is so important to engage fathers not living with their children. Barriers to engaging separated fathers within services will then be addressed, followed by a range of approaches for working with and supporting them in their relationships with children. A focus on the specific issues involved in working with young and separated fathers will be introduced and finally, an overview of possible approaches by individual services will be presented. The chapter concludes with some general suggestions about agency readiness in this important area.

Why is it important to engage separated fathers?

Due to significant rises in divorce rates in recent years, we know that children now live in a range of family structures within the UK. Of the 12 million children in England and Wales, more than one in four have separated parents (Her Majesty's Government, 2004). Although the number of lone fathers has nearly tripled in the last 40 years, 90% of lone-parent families are largely headed by mothers, with 89% of non-resident parents being fathers (Office for National Statistics, 2007).

It is now well known that unfortunately, there can be a wide range of poorer outcomes associated with family breakdown, such as lower educational achievement, a greater likelihood of living in poverty and of experiencing difficulties in the areas of mental health and emotional stability. Since nearly a quarter of children in the UK live in lone-parent families (Office for National Statistics: *Social Trends*, 2007), this is an extremely important issue for services to address. Five important factors have been identified which predict how well children do after their parents have separated:

- the quality of the children's relationship with their mothers
- the quality (not necessarily the quantity) of their relationship with their father
- how much and how badly the adults continue to argue
- the financial support available to children after separation
- the child's individual temperament.

(Lamb, 2002).

Flouri (2005) found that when non-resident fathers were highly involved with their children, this served to protect children against later mental-health problems. Despite the prevalence of separation, it is clear that mainstream early years services have not usually tackled separation issues either at a policy or practice level, especially regarding the child-father relationship.

It is important that when working with families we know to be separated, that services have a range of specific aims in mind, to help achieve the best possible outcomes for children. These might include the following:

- to retain as much parental and extended family support for children as possible (where safe to do so) including fathers and other family males

- to reduce children's experience of obstruction, conflict, and multiple life changes, supporting and challenging mothers and fathers where needed
- to increase children's experience of stability, compromise and resolution
- to proactively create an expectation of child-centred co-operation between separated mothers and fathers within services
- to take a child-centred, whole-family approach, and to meet The Gender Equality Duty (important because the early years workforce is predominantly female and traditionally works mainly through mothers)

Barriers to engaging separated fathers

As is highlighted in other chapters throughout this book, there are a wide range of general barriers to father inclusion in services, such as generally feminized environments and staffing, lack of service awareness of the importance of father involvement, lack of confidence in working with men, service delivery times, cultural and/or traditional beliefs in families about the fathering role and fathers' own lack of confidence in what they can offer to children and a reluctance to seek help. In relation to separated fathers there are clearly a number of additional barriers, relating to:

- the nature of the relationship between fathers and mothers following separation
- degree of access which fathers have to children after separation
- service lack of awareness of the importance of including separated fathers
- fathers' own lack of awareness of their importance to children after separation
- services not recognizing the need for separation-aware approaches
- geographical distance between fathers and children.

Services need to be aware of such challenges when attempting to provide support for this group of fathers.

Approaches

Being clear about the language

In order to work effectively in this complex field, it is vital that practitioners share a common understanding of what relevant terms mean as they relate to parents and families who have been separated. Below are some of the most relevant terms in use.

Separated parenting refers to any two people who do not live together but have had a mutually consented relationship of any amount of time that has produced one child or more.

Shared parenting refers to an approximately equal parenting role after separation. Mother and father spend substantial, but not necessarily equal, periods of time with their child. Both have a role in all aspects of the child's life. 'Co-parenting' is occasionally also used.

A resident parent: the parent whom the child lives with predominantly, either through agreement or due to a residence order from a court.

A non-resident parent: a parent who, for most of the time, does not live with their child or children.

> ***Please note:*** *practitioners should never use the term 'Absent parent'. It was coined by the Child Support Agency along with 'Parent with care' and implies that one cares about their child and the other does not. You are likely to alienate any father who hears you use these terms.*

First contact with separated fathers

When services first come into contact with fathers who are separated from their families, a number of important issues are likely to arise and it is important that practitioners understand what these might be and are prepared to address them. In the early stages of separation, clients will often feel the need to vent their feelings, and for fathers, this may be the first chance they have had. Remember that some men may present hurt as anger. These feelings need to be carefully distinguished from aggression, which may pose a risk. While allowing for some venting, it is good to retain some structure and time limits, and important to make sure that fathers are aware of any additional specialist help they may need, before the end of a first contact. Early actions would be likely to include supportive listening and exploring. Staff will need to spend a lot of time listening to men, initially, as they may need to tell their stories. Eventually, though, it will be important to bring fathers' attention around to the need to focus on the longer term, and outcomes for their children.

> **Key issues for reflection**
>
> - Does your agency recognize the challenges involved in first contacts with separated fathers?
> - Does staff training address this particular situation?

Assessment principles and referral systems

When separated fathers come into contact with services, it is important that services are aware of the particular needs of this group of men, as they will clearly be different from resident fathers. One of the major strategies for ensuring that their needs are best assessed and addressed is the use of 'separation aware' paperwork. Essentially, this means the use of forms and systems which seek to recognize and address separated fathers' issues from a range of perspectives.

The following are examples of the kinds of things we need to ask about and pass on, if we want to support separated families and the child-father relationship within them:

- Is this a separated family?
- What is the level of conflict or co-operation and from whom? (Usually based on subjective opinion – whose? Keep an open mind).
- Is the resident parent attempting to overly restrict the child's relationship with the non-resident parent?
- Is there a way of positively involving a parent who is not currently involved (usually a non-resident father)? What are their contact details?
- Are there any court orders in place or concerns about safety for children and mothers that limit the possibilities?
- Are there any pressing issues that need immediate action?

As well as the usual range of family support, the following are agencies which may be useful to refer fathers on to:

- **Families Need Fathers** support and the best information for non-resident or excluded fathers, mothers and grandparents on a whole range of needs including seeking and enforcing contact.
- **Family Mediation** – for trying to resolve disagreements without going to court.
- **Family Law solicitors** – for seeking and enforcing contact.
- **MATCH** for non-resident mothers.

Clients with specific legal needs should of course be referred to specialist help, but you may need to give them a sense of the possibilities. If you need specific advice about the legal aspects of your own work with a separated family, consult your line manager or your agency's separation policy.

As we build separation awareness into our ongoing work, we may choose different methods and actions depending on the kind of clients and families we are working with. Let's look at some of the ways that might work.

Key issues for reflection

- Does your agency ask you to record the separation status of clients (typically mothers), the contact details of non-resident parents (usually fathers), and the existence of contact and other orders in paperwork and referrals?
- If not, how could your systems be most easily modified to allow for this?

Working with separated mothers

That's right – looking at working with mothers, *before* we go on to fathers – in a book about fathers! Here's why:

As we saw in Chapter 5, the early years sector is staffed mainly by women, and traditionally delivers services mainly through women. Resident mothers will likely be your first point of contact with a separated family. Unless you suggest fathers' involvement as a positive for the children, and ask for their contact details, it is unlikely that you will even meet many non-resident fathers (Equal Opportunities Commission (EOC), 2007).

There is also strong evidence that the attitude of the resident parent and the friendliness between parents is the greatest predictor of continued father involvement:

- 64% of non-resident fathers were still in contact when their child was 9–10 months old, but this was highly correlated with the nature of the relationship between the parents. Where the mother had a very friendly relationship with the father, 94% of fathers were very interested in their child, compared with only 26% of fathers being very interested where the parents were unfriendly.
- Just over a third of in-contact absent fathers saw their 9–10-month-old child daily, and the level of contact rose the more interested he was in the child and the better his relationship with the mother.

Taking the vital step of talking to mothers explicitly about separation means we can help them consider the long-term importance for children of fathers (and their extended family) – at a time when frustration, anger and hurt may make it harder for them to remember the bigger picture for their children.

Where mothers feel the father is incompetent or unmotivated, it may reassure them to feel that someone is helping them to develop their parenting skills. Arranging contact in a supportive high-quality setting like a children's centre 'Stay and Play' session for example can help to reassure mothers and build their confidence in the father.

Because we have asked about separation, we may be able to relate it to changes in the children's behaviour. We may be able to pick up on conflict affecting children and help families towards co-operation.

Where young mothers are living with, or have close support and childcare from their own mother, the maternal grandparents can sometimes act as gatekeepers, acting, as they see it, in the best interests of their daughter. It can also be very useful to engage them in a conversation about the long-term needs of the child.

An important approach to persuading mothers to engage with their separated partner is to discuss with them the many potential benefits of doing so. One of the most significant issues here is that there is an under-used child-care resource in non-resident fathers. Only around 1 in 8 employed lone mothers used the non-resident father for childcare ('Fathers and the Modern Family' – an analysis of the Millennium Cohort Surveys (MCS) commissioned by the Equal Opportunities Commission 2007a), although Gregg and Washbrook (2003) found that where mothers of very young children are employed full-time, substantial care by fathers did not have any negative impact on children.

There is also evidence that some resident mothers tend to receive more money from fathers when there is more contact and involvement:

- Where fathers were in contact, rates of paying maintenance were far higher for fathers who had an interest in their child (59%) than for those who had little interest (33%).
- Similarly, rates of payment were higher the friendlier the father's relationship with the mother, and where there was a higher frequency of contact between the father and child: 63% who saw their child daily paid maintenance compared with 32% who saw the child less than weekly.
(From 'Fathers and the Modern Family' – an analysis of the Millennium Cohort Surveys (MCS) commissioned by the Equal Opportunities Commission 2007a.)

Now let's look at how we might work with separated fathers themselves.

Understanding non-resident fathers

There are a number of key ideas and issues which we, as practitioners, need to bear in mind when working with non-resident fathers, especially where there are particular challenges inherent in their individual situations.

Key ideas:

- Separated fathers are parents like any other – avoid assumptions and only give advice where needed.
- Listen, encourage, inform, and where necessary, challenge.
- Help fathers take a long-term, child-centred view.
- Help fathers to communicate with the other parent in a way that minimizes conflict.
- Help fathers to make the most of contact (in whatever form) for young children.
- Help fathers to keep their emotions regarding the separation separate from their parental behaviour.

Fathers in low-conflict separations who see a lot of their children may simply have the normal needs of any early years parent. Non-resident fathers (and mothers) who have experienced conflict or obstruction to the child's relationship with them may need a lot of support, and typically report some of the following:

- initial shock and anger at not being able to see their children every day
- grief, which may be long-term
- high stress levels, especially if going through the courts to obtain contact or the situation suddenly changes
- high levels of frustration and hurt, which can be long-term and feel 'toxic'
- sometimes feeling like giving up on seeing the children:
  - for emotional protection – it is just too hard
  - because they feel like an undervalued 'spare part'
  - or because they may feel it will spare the children conflict
- having contact arrangements changed or cancelled at the last minute, particularly if they or the resident parent begins seeing a new partner
- a roller-coaster of emotions in switching parenting emotions on and off for contact, which can feel more charged for the child as a consequence
- supervised contact, which is a difficult experience
- periods when they have not been able to see their child. For some this may be protracted or even permanent.

Additional barriers for separated fathers can include:

- Mixed messages: he may perceive that mothers want help – but also want to retain 'ownership' of children. It is harder to be a confident, equal parent in a short time (four days a month is common).

- He may not know what a positive long-term benefit he could be to his children, even when separated, as fathers rarely get the chance to discuss fatherhood.
- Sense of injustice. The father may have a perception that he has not been listened to by services or treated fairly as a parent (including in the legal system) because of his gender. He may feel it unfair that he has been scrutinized, whereas the mother's new partner may not have been.

In these kinds of situations, practitioners will need to explore with fathers the best ways of communicating with the mother, such as those suggested below:

- being positive, behaving well and sharing information about the child, even if the resident parent doesn't – it is a good model for the child
- limiting it to parenting issues (not unsolvable adult relationship issues)
- never discussing anything problematic in front of, or in hearing of, the child
- not calling round uninvited, and limiting phone calls to agreed times
- writing letters as a more controllable method (and keeping a copy). The tone should be neutral and child-centred, concentrating on the outcomes for the child, not the writer's needs or feelings.
- Suggesting mediation or Relate counselling if communication about children becomes problematic

Changeovers

Changeovers are traditionally a time when conflict occurs. Parents can be encouraged to keep it simple and positive, saving anything else for discussion when the children cannot hear or see, even if the other parent doesn't. If changeovers are so problematic that they threaten contact, explore possible neutral changeover venues, like Contact Centres or children's centres.

Key issues for reflection

- Do you have guidelines about how to respond in the context of your work if parental conflict arises in a separated family?
- If not, how could such guidance be developed?

Improving direct contact for fathers and children

Another key area for discussion with separated fathers is how to make their parenting time with children (if available) natural and positive. Practitioners could explore a number of issues with men to support them in the development of their future relationship with their child/children, such as those suggested below.

What kind of time? Time with the parent needs to be relaxed. It doesn't have to be filled with treats and excitement. Talking and listening, attention, praise, reassurance, hugs and affection are more important to young children. They need routines and rituals, so using the same toys, games and bedtime routine can be important in creating stability. Fathers are important educators, so literacy and numeracy games and encouraging talking and questioning are great. Teaching children how to eat cheaply and healthily is also very useful for them, rather than assuming they need expensive treats.

Use children's centres. Their 'Stay and Play' sessions are ideal for building up and normalizing contact – no one else needs to know, and they may be able to arrange handovers. Non-resident parents can also pick up on lots of good ideas from other parents and staff, access courses, and reduce their isolation. Parent workers can interface between parents and others. Children's centres may also run father-only groups and activities which also can provide significant peer support for men.

Other things to do: Trips to beaches, parks and county fairs are good, weather permitting. Many museums and galleries are often free and many have play activities and family sessions. Matinées at cinemas and theatres are cheaper. Swimming pools, restaurant chains etc. sometimes offer family deals or 'children go free' – have a look at their website, call their head office or visit www.moneysavingexpert.com to see what's available.

Children's clothes, equipment, toys, games and books can be had at second-hand shops, the library, toy library, and play-resource centres. An age-/stage-appropriate range of things to play with, do, read and make, particularly together are more important than things being new.

Practical help with long-distance contact on a low budget: The costs of maintaining contact can be high, particularly when travelling some distance to maintain staying in contact. This can be prohibitive, involving travel, accommodation and meals out over and above ordinary parenting costs. This can prevent non-resident fathers (and mothers) on a low income from seeing their children.

- **Travel:** Coaches are usually cheaper than trains. Buying tickets in advance, and travelling off-peak is cheaper. If the resident parent is flexible, contact can be arranged around cheap tickets – for example avoiding expensive dates and times of day for handovers.
- **Accommodation:** Youth hostels have family rooms and cots if requested and you can cook. Camping is cheapest but you need to be well organized to keep young children comfortable. Families Need Fathers local groups sometimes offer bed and breakfast to parents and children – contact the branch in the area being visited to find out if anything is available.
- **Meals:** All youth hostels have cooking facilities. Picnics are fun and economic and if the weather's bad, have one indoors.

Ideas to support indirect contact: Even parents with regular direct contact may need ideas for maintaining the relationship between contact visits – two weeks is a very long time for young children. Some parents are limited to indirect contact only. In either case, it requires some co-operation from the resident parent, especially in the early years, as even with a court order indirect contact is easy to prevent. Ideas include:

- **Regular phone calls to children** are a very important form of contact, handled in an age-/development-appropriate way at times agreed with the resident parent. Out-of-school talking with parents is evidenced to be very important for children's educational and emotional development (Desforges and Abouchaar, 2003). Even once they have begun talking, children 0–5 are unlikely to be able to converse for long, but even before that, hearing their parent's voice regularly is reassuring.
- With 0–2s, just saying 'Good night', and 'I love you', can mean a lot to children.
  - Asking simple questions (not about the other parent) but being ready to do most of the talking, jotting a few reminders if needed about things you have seen or done is useful.
  - Reading out story books, and singing songs together.
  - Being silly, e.g. 'I am sending you a kiss – it is going out through my letterbox, down the road, onto the bus, it's coming up your street (etc.) and on to your cheek – mwa!' Finish with a phone hug with an appropriate sound effect as if you can feel them squeezing you.
- **Recording stories for bedtime onto CD, MP3, Smartphone etc.**
- **Sending drawn pictures, stickers and photos.** Copies can be in a scrapbook for the child to see when they are grown up, in case they are not passed on by the resident parent.

Working with young separated fathers

It is important to proactively engage separated young fathers to help maximize the long-term support they can give their children. While the long-term benefits to children are well evidenced, there are many practical and cultural difficulties for young separated fathers to overcome. Peer pressure to concentrate on having a good time, and a lack of knowledge about how to seek contact can be compounded if agencies are not welcoming or assume that separated young fathers are not interested in their children, or identify too closely with young women at the expense of children's wider needs (see Chapter 7 for more information on working with young fathers). In some cases the young father will be the more capable and confident parent, and it is vital to recognize this rather than automatically looking to professionals for support and childcare.

It is important to find out the father's contact details if you are initially working with the mother, and this in itself may be difficult, particularly if the maternal family is very protective. But it is also important that we contact young fathers directly, and advertise generally that our services are for them too, so that they can contact us.

It is unlikely that a young man leaving home due to family breakdown will find child-friendly accommodation, in which case he may need help finding a venue for contact to take place. If he is experiencing obstruction to contact, he may need supporting through the process of seeking contact. Whether actually needed or not, parenting courses and evidence of skills relevant to childcare, like cooking and budgeting, can be useful in reassuring mothers, grandmothers and the courts that he is taking his role seriously and the young child is safe with him – though young men may be offended if they feel they already have these abilities.

It can be counter-productive for young parents to have tenancies before they are ready, as unpaid rent and debts can have ongoing repercussions. If accommodation is not suitable, children's centres or grandparents' homes can be used for contact in the meantime. What solution will provide the most long-term stability for the child?

Supporting fathers whose contact with their children is supervised

In the context of separation, fathers can sometimes have to go through a period of supervised or supported contact because of allegations from the other parent. If these are unfounded it can be a particularly difficult time.

Practitioners will need to employ a range of strategies in such situations, as suggested below:

- Acknowledge the unpleasantness of being watched and anger at having to be checked up on when the other parent (or other adults in the child's life like step-parents) may not.
- Go through how it is working and discuss any pressure points and how they might be resolved.
- If needed, explore how to play and talk with the children, concentrating on them rather than the situation and keeping the long-term goal in view.
- Reassure them that anecdotally, an estimated 4 out of 5 parents successfully complete supervised contact and go on to unsupervised, informal contact.
- Where desired, identify suitable mainstream sessions at a children's centre which would provide a safe next step should the process be successful.

For parents who are unable to obtain direct contact of any kind, suggest they keep a scrapbook or diary with words and pictures for the child to see at some point in the future. This should perhaps be about love and thought for the child rather than a blow-by-blow account of the rights and wrongs of the situation. Explanations of what happened might be best in a separate letter.

Having explored a range of strategies for working with separated fathers by theme, we will now go on to consider issues for particular early years services in relation to including this group of parents.

Ideas by sector in a nutshell

Maternity

- Sigle-Rushton, Hobcraft and Kiernan (2005) found that being the formally recorded father was a strong predictor of the father's future contact with, and involvement in, their child's life. This suggests that simple practices like maternity and health visiting services actively encouraging the recording of biological fathers on birth certificates can improve outcomes.
- Inviting separated fathers to an antenatal class session put on specifically to explore early fatherhood will engage them early.
- Some separated fathers attend the birth where things are amicable. Mothers can be encouraged to provide very early contact to ensure child–father bonding.

Health visiting

Where co-operation is good, invite the father to your home visits. Metzl (1980) found that intellectual gains in 6-month-old infants were greater when both mothers and fathers were trained in infant-communication.

A secure attachment with the father is an important protective factor against disturbance in children whose mother suffers from a mental illness, including post-natal depression (Hall, 2004). Reassure mothers about the benefits of non-resident fathers providing support and child care – no one can take away from their importance as a mother, but fathers often provide usefully different things.

Children's centres/preschool

Mainstream stay and plays add a lot to ordinary contact, but separated fathers need to know they are for them. Advertising Saturday parent-and-child sessions for working non-resident parents is very useful, for example.

Liaise with local Cafcass/social care to explore possible co-operation, e.g.:

- special sessions for informally supervised contact
- next-step sessions after supervised contact
- handover services to avoid parental conflict before and after contact.

Invite non-resident fathers to parenting courses. Delivering a parent-education programme to both parents is 'significantly more effective' than delivering it to just one (Bakernans-Kranenburg et al., 2003).

Social care/adult services/services for young people

When working with resident parents who are struggling to cope, make relationships with the non-resident parent before a crisis arises. That way, if respite care is required, the parent and their extended family can provide it, thus giving the child more continuity and avoiding the need to use temporary carers.

Making my organization 'separation ready'

To conclude this chapter, we will now suggest a range of steps which services can take to better equip them to deal as effectively as possible with fathers who are separated from their children.

The following are steps which agencies can take to be effective at maximizing support for children after separation:

1 **Train and require staff to proactively address separation issues with clients**, prioritizing child-centred co-operation and the retention of both parents and their

extended families **as support for children**. Managers and frontline staff should have a working knowledge of practical and emotional separation issues, promote child-centred co-operation and be ready to attempt to address potential conflict. They should understand how to signpost appropriately to separation-specific organizations, and work jointly with a range of agencies if needed.

2 **Take a child-centred, whole-family approach** rather than identifying mainly with a presenting parent. Services should be welcoming and promote their service actively to both parents and their extended and stepfamilies as potential support for children.

3 **Meet the Gender Equality Duty (GED)** in their work. Services should differentiate and meet the needs of male and female service users and take positive action as suggested in GED guidelines to promote a workforce that reflects target clientele, rather than being predominantly single gender.

4 **Have a separation policy**, which is clear, simple and promoted to service users and staff. This details what parents and children can expect to happen in separation-specific circumstances like pick-up and drop-off, involvement in events and decision-making regarding children, what information about children will be shared and with whom, limits and exceptions and dispute resolution.

5 **Have paperwork and systems that are separation inclusive**. Record keeping, referrals, enrolments etc. include space for:
   a contact details for both biological parents and other significant carers,
   b important information like parental responsibility, court orders and residence status,
   c contact relationships,
   d a way of mapping child-parent relationships in complex blended families.

6 **Share information about children** (not about adults), and decision-making about children, with anyone known to be a parent and with anyone known to have Parental Responsibility – unless this is specifically excluded by a court or care order, or is proven to be a risk to the child or someone close to them. Where there is conflict, an objection from a parent without supporting evidence would not normally in itself be sufficient reason to exclude the other parent.

7 **Have robust risk-management processes on a case-by-case basis**. These are tuned to the particular challenges of separation, and distinguish risk to children from risk to other adults. They are creative with identifying child-centred ways of working with highly conflicted families and parents with complex issues, and challenge mothers and fathers equally.

8 **Listen to separated family members, and adjust their services in response to their needs**. This includes children, fathers, mothers (resident and 'non-resident') and those with complex needs.

Summary

Key themes from this chapter are:

- Family breakdown can lead to a range of poorer outcomes for children.
- It is therefore important for services to provide support to separated fathers to help to maintain positive relationships with, and outcomes for, children.
- One of the most important ways in which services can begin to support this group of fathers is to be 'separation aware' in terms of assessment, referral and approach.
- Services will need to work with both fathers and mothers to achieve positive relationships between all family members.
- First steps to becoming separation aware include: staff training in separation awareness and developing a separation policy.

Conclusion and Ways Forward

There is now widespread acceptance that fathers matter to outcomes for children and families, as a result of the compelling evidence base which has been developed over the last 30 years. We have made the case that it is especially important to engage fathers in the early years because it leads to an increased probability of continued and sustained father involvement throughout their child's development and education. We would emphasize that many of the issues and approaches outlined in this book will also be relevant to those working with fathers of older children.

As a result of an increasing focus on the importance of fathers, governments in the UK and beyond now recognize the necessity of providing support to fathers in their parenting role. This has led to a number of policy and statutory frameworks requiring public-sector services to engage with fathers and male carers. However, as has been demonstrated throughout this book, at present, universal father inclusion largely remains an aspiration rather than a reality. There are a number of reasons for this, including the often feminized nature of early years services, the attitudes and beliefs of practitioners, lack of training in working with men and structural issues in terms of service delivery (Monday – Friday, 9–5).

We have argued that agencies seeking to engage fathers in their work often lack the infrastructures to do so. The lack of father-friendly/male-friendly infrastructure is impacting upon all elements of the systems that surround children and families. If early years services and early years practitioners do not develop appropriate systems then they cannot effectively work with men. Previous chapters have outlined ideas regarding the necessary steps involved in developing such an infrastructure and these are summarized below.

Raising staff awareness

The first step is to raise awareness of the importance of fathers to children and families through staff training which allows staff to reflect upon and actively discuss the issues. Training needs to address the fact that everyone has experience of being fathered or not and that these experiences may well impact on their professional approach. Within this training, obligations on services to work with fathers need to be presented to trigger a discussion on what the service's current status is with regard to engaging fathers and what steps need to be taken to further develop that work. In order to ensure that all issues are fully discussed and their implications appreciated, training should be led by experts in the field of father inclusion, where possible.

Developing a position statement

Once staff at all levels of the service are aware of the importance of working with fathers/male carers, then a position statement should be developed, setting out clearly the service's vision and goals in relation to working with fathers/male carers, as discussed in Chapter 2. This statement should be widely disseminated, discussed and understood so that it becomes an active document which impacts on everyday practice. A timetable to implement and review change should be an integral part of this process. In all policy and marketing material, the term 'mothers and fathers' should be used in preference to 'parents', since, as we have argued throughout this book, fathers must be made much more visible to services and fathers themselves must be given to understand that services are available to them, as well as to mothers.

Developing father-inclusive information systems

As we saw in Chapter 3, it is vital that systems are in place to collect information on fathers, as soon as any service comes into contact with a family. Knowing who and where fathers are, is the very first step on the road to being able to offer men services.

Appointing fathers champions

The next step within the process of developing father-inclusive service might be to appoint 'fathers champions' in early years agencies, as has been discussed in several chapters in the book (see Chapter 7, for example). The prime task of this champion is to maintain a focus on father inclusion. Whenever work or activities are being planned or proposed, the fathers champion will ask: 'how do fathers fit into this?' It is a powerful question that leads practitioners and the team to actively consider the impact of their work with fathers. The champion's other task is to promote an ongoing awareness and understanding of the service's position statement in relation to working with fathers/male carers.

Adopting a gender-differentiated approach

As has been argued throughout the book, there is a need for a gender-differentiated approach to working with men which acknowledges that the needs of men and women are likely to be different and that these needs will need to be addressed differently. Such an approach is widely accepted as being most effective in engaging fathers/male carers and a number of case-study practice examples demonstrating this have been provided in previous chapters. For example, in Chapter 5, Tim Kahn discussed language use with mothers and fathers, with some words and phrases more likely to appeal to men than women and Chapters 6 and 7 examined the kinds of activities which are more likely to appeal to fathers/male carers, such as making bird boxes and dens. By developing such male-orientated services, it is much more likely that effective and meaningful work with fathers can take place.

Another important aspect of a gender-differentiated approach can be the appointment of a dedicated 'Fathers Worker' to engage fathers in services. This can be a very useful way of proceeding and we saw the benefits of such an approach in Chapter 6 where a skilled Fathers Worker was able to engage a number of fathers in an early years transitions project, in an area where fathers had rarely been engaged with service before. It is important to stress here that Fathers Workers do not have to be male. What matters most in engaging fathers are the skills and abilities of the worker and women can be highly effective in such an endeavour (see Potter and Carpenter, 2008, for example). However, a possible difficulty with the use of a dedicated

Fathers Worker is that it can lead to a belief amongst the rest of the team that anything relating to fathers is the sole remit of the dedicated worker. This will ultimately be unproductive, as the whole team has to take responsibility for working with fathers, if the service is to be fully inclusive. There is also the real risk that when the dedicated Fathers Worker moves on, the work with fathers falls to the ground. In order to avoid such a scenario, the key role of a Fathers Worker should not only be to work directly with fathers and men but also to enable the whole team and the whole system to work with fathers and men.

A further approach which some services have adopted, in the context of a gender-differentiated approach, is the setting up of 'dads groups' which are exclusively for men. These groups are needed and can be extremely effective in drawing men in who have not used services before, as we saw in Chapters 6 and 7. They have their place but agencies need to be aware that establishing a 'dads group' should constitute only the first step on what is likely to be a long road towards wider inclusion: it should not be an end in itself.

Recognizing diversity

Part Three of the book draws attention to the issue that fathers are not a homogenized group and that issues of diversity must be recognized and addressed to include all fathers in services. Fathers, like mothers, will have a range of experiences and needs related to age, ability/disability, type of family background, employment and economic status, religious and cultural values and beliefs and sexual orientation, among others. Fatherhood presents itself in many forms and practitioners offering a 'one size fits all' approach will experience difficulties in engaging many men. Fathers have a range of distinctive needs and require services to meet those needs because we know that a father's behaviour, beliefs and aspirations can profoundly influence the health and well-being of both mother and child in positive and negative ways and the need to support men in their parenting role is of crucial importance to families.

Working with mothers

Throughout this book, the importance of mothers' contribution to child and family well-being has been emphasized, along with the necessity of working with and through mothers to engage men. In Chapter 6, we saw that the Fathers Worker engaged in almost as much follow-up contact with mothers, as with fathers. Mothers are much more likely to be experienced service users and their support and persuasion will almost certainly be essential, if men are to take the significant step towards service use themselves.

Service monitoring and evaluation

A father-inclusive service infrastructure will also require an on-going process of evaluation. Chapter 3 discusses the need for father-inclusive data-collection systems, arguing that it is essential to record all instances of father/male carer engagement/attendance, to help agencies determine how effective its work with men actually is. If no record is kept of father attendance across services, how will they know if they are making progress towards a goal of father inclusion? Some key questions for regular evaluations are:

- Is the number of fathers using our service increasing?
- To what extent are we engaging fathers with a diverse range of backgrounds over time: young fathers, fathers from minority ethnic backgrounds, fathers of disabled children and separated fathers?
- What kinds of services are being accessed and which are not?
- What may be preventing fathers from accessing services?
- What do fathers think about our services?
- How involved are fathers in the development of our services?
- How will we further develop the process of recruitment and retainment to engage more men?

Including fathers across the full range of early years services may seem a daunting task, requiring a significant investment of commitment, time, training and resources. However, fathers matter very much to the well-being and development of children and families and it is therefore imperative that services develop approaches which can actively support them in their parenting role. Such a goal is now enshrined in UK public-sector policy but much more needs to be done to translate these aspirations into practice. We hope that the current volume may contribute towards a greater understanding of what is involved in making progress towards the ultimate goal of father-inclusive services in the early years and beyond.

Appendix: Policy and Statutory Frameworks

1 The Framework for the Assessment of Children in Need and their Families (DH, 2000)
2 The Children Act (1989, 2004)
3 The National Service Framework for Children, Young People and Maternity Services: Core Standards (DH/DfES, 2004)
4 Engaging Fathers: Involving Parents, Raising Achievement (DfES, 2004)
5 Working Together to Safeguard Children (2006)
6 Routine post-natal care of women and their babies (NICE, 2006)
7 The Equality Act (2006)
8 Sure Start Children's Centres: Practice Guidance (DfES, 2006, 2007)
9 Sure Start Children's Centres: Planning and Performance Management Guidance (DfES, 2006, 2007)
10 Gender Equality Duty and Local Government: Guidance for Public Authorities in England (EOC, 2007)
11 Maternity Matters (DH, 2007)
12 Every Parent Matters (DfES 2007)
13 Aiming High for Children: Supporting Families (HM Treasury/DfES, 2007)
14 The Children's Plan (DCSF, 2007)
15 Teenage Parenting Strategy and Guidance (DCSF, 2007, 2008)
16 Teenage Pregnancy Independent Advisory Group Annual Report (2008)
17 Children and Young People's Workforce Strategy (DCSF, 2008)
18 SCIE guidelines for supporting parents (2008)
19 The Welfare Act (2009)
20 The Childcare Strategy (DWP, HM Treasury, DCSF, Cabinet Office, 2009)
21 Healthy lives, brighter futures: the strategy for children and young people's health (DCSF, DH, 2009)
22 Getting Maternity Services Right for teenage mothers and young fathers (DH, DCSF, 2009)

23 The Healthy Child Programme (DH, Update 2009)
24 Support for All (Green Paper on families) (DCSF, 2010)
25 Teenage Pregnancy Strategy: beyond 2010 (DCSF, DH, 2010)
26 Maternity and Early Years: making a good start to family life (DH, DCSF, 2010)
27 Parenting and Family Support: guidance for Local Authorities in England (DCSF, 2010)
28 Supporting Families in the Foundation Years (DfE, 2011).

References

Acheson, D. (1998) *Independent Enquiry into Inequalities in Health Report.* London: The Stationery Office.

Bakermans-Kraneburg, M. J., Van Ijzendoorn, M. H. and Juffer, F. (2003) 'Less is more: Meta-analyses of sensitivity and attachment interventions in early childhood'. *Psychological Bulletin,* 129, 195–215.

Barn, R., Ladino, C. and Rogers, B. (2006) *Parenting in Multi-racial Britain.* York: Joseph Rowntree Foundation.

Barnes, J., Ball, M., Meadows, P., Belsky, J. and the FNP Implementation Research Team (2009) *Nurse Family Partnership Programme. Second Year Pilot Sites Implementation in England. The Infancy Period.* Birkbeck College. London: DCSF.

Barter, C., McCarry, M., Berridge, D. and Evans, K. (2009) *Partner Exploitation and Violence in Teenage Intimate Relationships.* London: NSPCC.

Bavolek, S. J. (1990) *The Art and Science of Raising Healthy Children.* http://www.nurturingparenting. com/research_validation/art_and_science_of_raising_healthy_children.pdf

Beresford, B., Rabiee, P. and Sloper, P. (2007) *Priorities and Perceptions of Disabled Children and Young People and their Parents Regarding Outcomes from Support Services.* York: Social Policy Research Unit, University of York.

Blanden, J. (2006) *'Bucking the trend': What Enables those who are Disadvantaged in Childhood to Succeed Later in Life?* London: Department of Work and Pensions.

Bowlby, J. (1953) *Child Care and the Growth of Love.* London: Penguin Books.

Burgess, A. (2006) 'Young Fathers'. *Working With Young Men,* 5, 2, 13–17.

—(2008) *The Costs and Benefits of Active Fatherhood* which can be downloaded from the Fatherhood Institute website: www.fatherhoodinstitute.org

Burgess, A. and Bartlett, D. (2004) *Working with Fathers: a Guide for Everyone Working with Families.* London: Fathers Direct.

Burgess, A. and Ruxton, S. (1996) *Men and their Children.* London: IPPR.

Cameron, C., Mooney, A. and Moss, P. (2002) 'The child care workforce: current conditions and future directions'. *Critical Social Policy,* 22, 4, 572–95.

Carpenter, B. (2002) 'Inside the portrait of a family: the importance of fatherhood'. *Early Child Development and Care,* 172, 2, 195–202.

Children's Workforce Development Council (2010) *The State of the Children's and Young People's Data Review.* Available at http://www.cwdcouncil.org.uk/workforce-data/state-of-the-young-peoples-workforce-report (accessed July, 2011).

Commission for Healthcare Audit and Inspection (2008) *Towards Better Births.* Available at http://www.cqc.org.uk/_db/_documents/Towards_better_births_200807221338.pdf (accessed 13/6/11).

Contact a Family (n.d.) *Fathers.* Available at: http://www.cafamily.org.uk/pdfs/fathers.pdf

Cullen, S., Cullen, M., Band, S., Davis, L. and Lindsay, G. (2011) 'Supporting fathers to engage with their children's learning and education: an under-developed aspect of the Parent Support Adviser pilot'. *British Educational Research Journal,* 37, 3, 485–500.

Department for Children, Schools and Families (1989, 2004) *The Children Act.* London: The Stationery Office.

—(2007a) *Engaging Effectively with Black and Minority Ethnic Parents in Children's and Parental Services.* London: The Stationery Office.

—(2007b) *The Children's Plan.* London: The Stationery Office.

—(2007c) *Teenage Parents Next Steps: Guidance for Local Authorities and Primary Care Trusts.* London: The Stationery Office.

—(2008) *Analysing Child Deaths and Serious Injury through Abuse and Neglect – What can we Learn? A Biennial Analysis of Serious Case Reviews 2003–05.* London: The Cabinet Office.

—(2009a) *The Dads Test Guide.* Available at http://www.surreycc.gov.uk/education/sbdb.nsf/a5d81c5944427897802569a8005ace46/608cb92816fe7b568025766a004e45c4/$FILE/09-FS-210a.pdf (accessed 10/6/11).

—(2009b) *Think Family Toolkit – Improving Support for Families at Risk.* Available at https://www.education.gov.uk/publications/standard/publicationdetail/page1/DCSF-00685-2009.

—(2009c) *Involving Parents, Raising Achievement, Healthy Lives, Brighter Futures: the Strategy for Children and Young People's Health.* London: The Stationery Office.

—(2010a) *Think Family.* London: The Stationery Office.

—(2010b) *Think Family Service (Guidance note 2).* London: The Stationery Office.

—(2010c) *Think Family Service.* London: The Stationery Office.

Department for Children, Schools and Families and Department of Health (2008) *Teenage parents: Who Cares?* A Guide to Commissioning and Delivering Maternity Services for Young Parents (2nd Edition). London: The Stationery Office.

—(2009) *Getting Maternity Services Right for Pregnant Teenagers* and 'Young Fathers' (revised edition). London: The Stationery Office.

Department for Education (2011) *Supporting Families in the Foundation years.* London: The Stationery Office.

Department for Education and Skills (2006–2007a) *Sure Start Children's Centres: Practice Guidance.* London: The Stationery Office.

—(2006–2007b) *Sure Start Children's Centres: Planning and Performance Management Guidance.* London: The Stationery Office.

—(2007) *Aiming High for Children: Supporting Families.* London: The Stationery Office.

—(2007) *Every Parent Matters.* London: The Stationery Office.

—(2010) *Sure Start Children's Centres: Performance, Achievements and Outcomes Review*. London: The Stationery Office.

Department of Health (2000) *The Framework for the Assessment of Children in Need and their Families*. London: HMSO.

—(2000) *Excellence Not Excuses: Inspection of Services for Ethnic Minority Children and Families*. London: DH Publications.

—(2007) *Our NHS, Our Future*. London: The Stationery Office.

—(2009) *The Healthy Child Programme: Pregnancy and the First Five Years of Life*. London: DH Publications.

—(2010) *Parents' Views on the Maternity Journey and Early Parenthood; What Expectant and New Parents have told us about their Experiences of Maternity and Early Years Care*. London: DH Publications.

Department of Health and Department for Education and Skills (2004) *National Service Framework for Children, Young People and Maternity Services*. London: DH Publications. Available at: http://www.dh.gov.uk/en/Publicationsandstatistics/Publications/PublicationsPolicyAndGuidance/DH_4089101.

Department of Health, Social Services and Public Safety (2009) *Racial Equality in Health and Social Care*. Equality Commission for Northern Ireland.

Desforges, C. and Abouchaar, A. (2003) *The Impact of Parental Involvement, Parental Support and Family Education on Pupil Achievement and Adjustment: A Literature Review*. Nottingham: DfES.

Dewar Research (2009). Government Statistics on Domestic Violence: *Estimated Prevalence of Domestic Violence*. England and Wales 1995–2009/09.

El-Sheikh, M. and Harger, J. (2001) 'Appraisals of marital conflict and children's adjustment, health, and physiological reactivity'. *Developmental Psychology*, 37, 875–85.

Equal Opportunities Commission (2007a) *Fathers and the Modern Family*. Available at: http://www.familieslink.co.uk/download/sept07/EOC%20version%20of%20fathers%20and%20the%20modern%20family.pdf (accessed 16/6/11).

—(2007b) *Gender Equality Duty and Local Government: Guidance for Public Authorities in England*. Available at http://www.equalityhumanrights.com/uploaded_files/PSD/the_gender_equality_duty_and_local_government_-_guidance_for_public_authorities.pdf

European Social Fund (2007) *Equality and Diversity Good Practice Guide – Ethnic Minority Communities*. European Social fund. Available at http://www.dwp.gov.uk/docs/age.pdf

Fabian, H. and Dunlop, A. (2006) *Outcomes of Good Practice in Transition Processes for Children Entering Primary School*. United Nations: Educational, Scientific and Cultural Organization.

Fagan, J. and Palm, G. (2004) *Fathers and Early Childhood Programs*. Canada: Delmar Learning.

Farmer, E. and Owen, M. (1998) 'Gender and the child protection process', *British Journal of Social Work*, 28, 1, 545–64.

Fatherhood Institute (2009) *Invisible Fathers: Working with Young Dads – a Resource Pack*. Abergavenny. Fatherhood Institute.

—(2010a) *Collecting Fathers' Contact Details: What the Law Says*. Available at http://www.fatherhoodinstitute.org/2010/collecting-fathers-contact-details-what-the-law-says/ (accessed 16/6/11).

—(2010b) *Research Summary: Muslim Fathers*. Available at http://www.fatherhoodinstitute.org/2010/ fatherhood-institute-research-summary-muslim-fathers/ (accessed in July 2011).

Fatherhood Institute Early Years Page: http://www.fatherhoodinstitute.org/index.php?id=3

Featherstone, B. (2009) *Contemporary Fathering: Theory, Policy and Practice*. Bristol: The Policy Press.

Fisher, D. (2007) *Including New Fathers: A Guide for Maternity Professionals*. London: The Fatherhood Institute. Available at: <http://www.fatherhoodinstitute.org/uploads/publications/ 246.pdf. Accessed 6/12/11>.

Fletcher, R. and Daley, K. (2002) 'Fathers' involvement in their children's literacy development'. *Evolving Literacies*. Perth: Australian Literacy Educators National Conference.

Flouri, E. (2005) *Fathering and Child Outcomes*. Chichester: Wiley.

Flouri, E. and Buchanan, A. (2001) 'Father time'. *Community Care*, 4–10 October, 42.

—(2003) 'What predicts father involvement with their children? A prospective study of intact families'. *British Journal of Developmental Psychology*, 21, 1, 81–98.

—(2004) 'Early father's and mother's involvement and child's later educational outcomes'. *British Journal of Educational Psychology*, 74, 2, 141–53.

Ghate, D., Shaw, C. and Hazel. N. (2000) *Engaging Fathers in Preventive Services: Fathers and Family Centres*. York: Joseph Rowntree Foundation.

Goldman, R. (2005) *Fathers' Involvement in their Children's Learning*. London: National Family and Parenting Institute.

Hall, A. (2004) 'Parental psychiatric disorder and the developing child'. In M. Gopfert, J. Webster and M. V. Seeman (eds), *Parental Psychiatric Disorder: Distressed Parents and their Families* (2nd ed.) Cambridge: Cambridge University Press.

Harrison, J., Henderson, M. and Leonard, R. (2007) *Different Dads: Fathers' Stories of Parenting Disabled Children*. London: Jessica Kingsley Publishers.

Hawkins, A. J. and Dollahite, D. C. (1997) *Generative Fathering: Beyond Deficit Perspectives*. Thousand Oaks, CA: Sage.

Henricson, C. (2001) *National Mapping of Family Services in England and Wales*. A consultation document. London: NFPI

HM Government (2010) *The Coalition: Our Programme for Government*. London: The Cabinet Office.

Holden, G. W. and Barker, T. (2004) 'Fathers in Violent Homes'. In M. E. Lamb ed. *The Role of the Father in Child Development*. London: Wiley.

Home Office (1998) *Supporting Families – A Consultation Document*. London: The Stationary Office.

Home Office Statistical Bulletin. 'Crime in England and Wales 2008/09'. Volume 1. *Findings from the British Crime Survey and Police Recorded Crime*.

Hornby, G. (1992) 'A review of fathers' accounts of their experiences of parenting children with disabilities'. *Disability, Handicap and Society*, 7, 4, 363–74.

Jekielek, S. M. (1998) Parental Conflict, Marital Disruption and Children's Emotional Well-Being. *Social Forces*, 76, 905–36.

Jones, E. and Ware, J. (1997) 'Early intervention services to children with special needs: a Welsh study'. In B. Carpenter ed. *Families in Context: Emerging Trends in Family Support and Early Intervention*. London: David Fulton.

Kahn, T. (2005) *Fathers' Involvement in Early Years Settings: Findings from Research*. London: Pre-school Learning Alliance. Available at: http://www.pre-school.org.uk/practitioners/research/353/fathers-involvement-in-early-years-settings).

—(2009) *The Dad Challenge*. London: Pre-school Learning Alliance. The summary and full report can be accessed at http://www.pre- school.org.uk/practitioners/inclusion/380/engaging-fathers

Khan, H. (2006) *In Conversation with Muslim Dads*. London: Fathers Direct/An-Nisa Society. Available at: www.fatherhoodinstitute.org/uploads/publications/268.pdf (accessed in July 2011).

Kiernan, K., & Smith, K. (2003) Unmarried parenthood: new insights from the Millenium Cohort Study. *Population Trends*, 114, 26–33. London: Office of Population, Censuses and Surveys.

Lamb, M. E. (2002) 'Placing children's interests first: developmentally appropriate parenting plans'. *The Virginia Journal of Social Policy and the Law*, 10, 98–119.

—ed. (2004) *The Role of the Father in Child Development*. 4th ed. New York: Wiley.

—(2010) *The Role of the Father in Child Development*. 5th ed. New Jersey: John Wiley and Sons.

Lamb, M. E. and Lewis, C. (2004) 'The development and significance of father-child relationships in two-parent families'. In M. E Lamb ed. *The Role of the Father in Child Development*. 4th ed. New York: Wiley.

—(2010) 'The development and significance of father-child relationships in two-parent families'. In M. E. Lamb ed. *The Role of the Father in Child Development*. 5th ed. London: Wiley.

Latif, S. (2010) *Effective Methods of Engaging Black and Minority Ethnic Communities within Healthcare Settings*. Race Equality Foundation Briefing Paper.

Lewis, C. and Lamb, M. E. (2007) *Fatherhood: Connecting the strands of diversity across time and space*. York: Joseph Rowntree Foundation. Available from http://www.jrf.org.uk/sites/files/jrf/understanding-fatherhood.pdf.

Lewis, J. (2002) 'The problem of fathers: policy and behaviour in Britain'. In B. Hodgson ed. *Making Men into Fathers: Men, Masculinities and the Social Politics of Fatherhood*. Cambridge: Cambridge University Press.

Lindfield, S. (2009) *Parenting Inside and Out: Bringing the Outside in. Developing a Family-Based Approach to Supporting Young Parents in Custody*. Brighton: Young People in Focus.

Lloyd, N., O'Brien, M. and Lewis, C. (2003) *Fathers in Sure Start*. London: National Evaluation of Sure Start.

Lloyd, T. (1994) 'Analysis of Newspaper Coverage of Fathers and Men as Carers'. Discussion Paper. London: Working with Men.

Macdonald, E. E. and Hastings, R. P. (2010) 'Fathers of children with developmental disabilities'. In M. E. Lamb ed. *The Role of the Father in Child Development*. 5th ed. London: John Wiley.

Macleod, F. (2000) 'Low attendance by fathers at family literacy events: some tentative explanations'. *Early Child Development and Care*, 161, 107–19.

McDonnell, E., Seabrook, A., Braye, S., Bridgeman, J. and Keating, K. (2009) *Talking Dads: Young Dads in Brighton and Hove Explore Parenthood*. Brighton: University of Sussex.

Mencap (2006). *Breaking Point – Families Still Need a Break*. London: Mencap.

Metzl, M. N. (1980) 'Teaching parents a strategy for enhancing infant developmen'. *Child Development*, 51, 2, 583–6.

Mirrlees-Black, C. (1999) *Domestic Violence: FIndings from a new British Crime Survey self-completion questionnaire*, Home Office Research Study 191. London: HMSO.

Mordaunt, E. (2005) *Young Fathers Project Evaluation Report*. Brighton: TSA.

National Audit Office (2006) *Sure Start Children's Centres*. London: NAO.

National Evaluation of Sure Start (2003) *Fathers in Sure Start*. London: Sure Start Unit.

Nursing and Midwifery Council Statistical analysis of the register 1 April 2006 to 31 March 2007.

Office for National Statistics (ONS) (2005) *Focus on Families*. Office for National Statistics.

—(2007) *Social Trends*.

—(2008) *Birth Statistics 2008, Series FM1. No 37*. Office for National Statistics. Newport.

Ofsted (2009) *The Evaluation Schedule for Schools*. Manchester: Crown Publications.

Page, J. and Whiting, G. (2007) *Engaging Effectively with Black and Minority Ethnic Parents in Children's and Parental Services*. Research Report 013. London: DCSF.

Page, J., Whitting, G. and McLean, C. (2008) *A Review of How Fathers Can be Better Recognized and Supported through DCSF Policy*. London: DCSF.

Pancsofar, N. and Vernon-Feagans, L. (2006) 'Mother and father language input to young children: Contributions to later language development'. *Journal of Applied Developmental Psychology, 27*, 571–87.

Parekh, A., Mcinnes, T. and Kenway, P. (2010) *Monitoring Poverty and Social Exclusion*. York: Joseph Rowntree Foundation.

Pelchat, D. and Lefebvre, H. L. N. (2004) 'A holistic intervention programme for families with a child with a disability'. *Journal of Advanced Nursing, 48*, 2, 124–31.

Pelchat, D., Lefebvre, H. L. N. and Perreault, M. (2003) 'Differences and similarities between mothers' and fathers 'experiences of parenting a child with a disability'. *Journal of Child Health Care, 7*, 231–47.

Pollock, S., Trew, R., and Jones, K. (2005) *Young Black Fathers and Maternity Services*. School of Policy Studies, University of Bristol. Available at www.fatherhoodinstitute.org/uploads/publications/186. pdf (accessed in July 2011).

Potter, C. and Carpenter, J. (2008) ' "Something in it for dads": getting fathers involved with Sure Start'. *Early Child Development and Care, 178*, 8, 761–72.

Potter, C. A., Walker, G. D. and Keen, B. (2009) *Father Involvement in Children's Early Learning Transitions*. Leeds Metropolitan University, Research report.

Quinton, D., Pollock, S., and Golding, J. (2002) *The Transition to Fatherhood in Young Men - Influences on Commitment*. ESRC report, available at www.regard.ac.uk.

Reeves, J. (2008) ed. *Inter-professional Approaches to Young Fathers*. Keswick: MandK Update Ltd.

Salway, S., Chowbey, P. and Clarke, L. (2009) *Parenting in Modern Britain – Understanding the Experiences of Asian Fathers*. York: Joseph Rowntree Foundation.

Sanders, A. et al. (2008) *Hard to Reach? Engaging with Fathers in Early Years Settings*. Derby: University of Derby and Pre-school Learning Alliance.

Sanders, D., White, G., Burge, B., Sharp, C., Eames, A., Mceune, R. and Grayson, H. (2005) *A Study of the Transition from the Foundation Stage to Key Stage 1*. London: National Foundation for Educational Research.

Sarkadi, A., Kristiansson, R., Oberklaid, F. and Bremberg, S. (2008) 'Fathers' involvement and children's developmental outcomes: a systematic review of longitudinal studies'. *Acta Paediatrica*, 97, 2, 153–8.

Seligman, M. and Darling, R. B. (2007) Ordinary Families: Special Children; A Systems Approach to Childhood Disability. *New York: The Guildford Press.*

SENSE (2001) 'A voice for fathers'. Available at: http://www.sense.org.uk/publicationslibrary/allpubs/talking_sense/children_families/fathers (accessed 21 April, 2011).

Sherriff, N. S. (2007) *Supporting Young Fathers: Examples of Promising Practice*. Brighton: Trust for the Study of Adolescence.

Sherriff, N. S. and Hall, V. (2011) 'Engaging and supporting fathers to promote breastfeeding'. *Scandinavian Journal of Caring Sciences.*

Sherriff, N. S, Hall, V., and Pickin, M. (2009) 'Fathers' perspectives on breastfeeding: ideas for intervention. *British Journal of Midwifery*, 17, 223–7.

Sigle-Rushton, W., Hobcraft, J. and Kiernan, K. (2005) 'Parental divorce and subsequent disadvantage: A cross-cohort comparison'. *Demography*, 42, 427–46.

Singh, D. and Newburn, M. (2000) *Becoming a Father: Men's Access to Information and Support about Pregnancy, Birth, and Life with a New Baby*. London: National Childbirth Trust.

Social Care Institute for Excellence (2005) *Being a Father to a Child with Disabilities: Issues and What Helps* (SCARE Briefing Report 16). [Online at: www.scie.org.uk]

Stanley, K. ed. (2005) *Daddy Dearest: Active Fatherhood and Public Policy*. London: Institute for Public Policy Research.

The Equality Act (2006) London: The Stationery Office.

The Stephen Lawrence Inquiry (1999) Report of an Inquiry by Sir William Macpherson of Cluny. Stationery Office.

Think Fathers http://www.think-fathers.org/

Towers, C. (2009) *Recognising Fathers: A National Survey of Fathers who have Children with Learning Disabilities*. London: Foundation for People with Learning Disabilities.

UN (2011) 'Men in Families and Family Policy in a Changing World'. New York: United Nations.

Warwick, I., Chase, E., Hollingworth, K., Simon, A. and Boyce, P. (2011) *Young Fatherhood: Roles, Expectations and Support*. London: Thomas Coram Research Unit.

Washbrook, E. (2007) *Fathers, Childcare and Children's Readiness to Learn*. Bristol: The Centre for Marketing and Public Organization.

West, S. (2000) *Just a Shadow: A Review of Support for the Fathers of Children with Disabilities*. Birmingham: The Handsel Trust.

White, M. (2010) 'Disadvantaged young fathers-to-be'. *The Psychologist*, 23, 3. 198–200.

Wolfberg, A. J. et al. (2004) 'Dads as breastfeeding advocates: results of a randomized controlled trial of an educational intervention'. *American Journal of Obstetrics and Gynecology*, 3, 191, 708–12.

Index